UNRESTRICTED:

A WOMAN'S GUIDE TO LEADING THROUGH LIMITATIONS

Liz St James

Published by Urban Cryo Publishing Inc.
A subsidiary of R&L St. James Holding Corp.
Synovial Space ™ is a registered trademark of H2P Collective Corp. Used under license.
ISBN: 979-8-218-89364-4
Cover design by Liz St James
For more information:
www.H2Pcollective.com
lstjames@h2pcollective.com
DISCLAIMER
The information in this book is provided for educational purposes only and is based on the author's personal and professional experience. It is not intended to be a substitute for professional medical, psychological, financial, or legal advice. Readers should consult with qualified professionals before making significant life changes.

Contents

Disclaimer

Please Read Carefully

The content in Unrestricted: A Woman's Guide to Leading Through Limitations is provided for educational and informational purposes only. It is based on the author's personal experiences over 20 years of hospitality leadership, life coaching training, and the Synovial Space methodology developed by Raphael St James.

This book is not a substitute for professional medical, psychological, financial, or legal advice.

Health and Medical Disclaimer

Liz St James is a life coach but not a licensed medical professional, therapist, psychiatrist, or psychologist. The personal health stories shared in this book—including pregnancy complications, hypertension, caregiving experiences, and mental health discussions—are based on individual experience and should not be interpreted as medical or psychological advice.

If you are experiencing physical health issues, mental health concerns, emotional distress, caregiver burnout, or any medical condition, consult with qualified healthcare providers before implementing any strategies from this book.

Crisis support: If you are in crisis, contact emergency services (911), the National Suicide Prevention Lifeline (988), or the Crisis Text Line (text HELLO to 741741) immediately.

Crisis Resources

- National Suicide Prevention Lifeline: 988

- Crisis Text Line: Text HELLO to 741741
- National Domestic Violence Hotline: 1-800-799-7233
- SAMHSA National Helpline: 1-800-662-4357
- Emergency Services: 911

Professional, Career, and Financial Disclaimer

The career guidance and financial concepts in this book are based on personal experience in hospitality leadership (2000–2025), entrepreneurship, and life coaching. The author is not a licensed career counselor, employment attorney, HR professional, financial advisor, or accountant.

Workplace laws, policies, and best practices vary by location, industry, and time period. Financial strategies must be tailored to individual circumstances.

Consult qualified professionals before making significant career or financial decisions, including those concerning:

- Legal workplace issues (discrimination, termination, contracts)
- Major career transitions or starting businesses
- Investment, debt management, or financial planning decisions

No income guarantees or financial outcomes are promised.

Synovial Space Methodology

The Synovial Space methodology was developed by Raphael St James based on his experience with osteoarthritis. It uses synovial fluid as a metaphor for creating movement within restrictions.

This methodology is:

- A framework for navigating life's restrictions
- An educational tool for personal development

This methodology is not:

- A medical treatment for physical conditions
- A replacement for therapy or medical care
- A guarantee of specific outcomes

No Guaranteed Results

While the author has found success using these frameworks—including career advancement, successful transitions, and co-founding H2P Collective Corp.—individual results will vary significantly.

Success depends on individual effort, personal circumstances, systemic factors, timing, resources, support systems, and countless variables beyond anyone's control.

The author and publisher make no guarantees regarding:

- Career advancement or professional success
- Financial outcomes or income generation
- Relationship improvements or personal fulfillment
- Physical health or mental wellness outcomes
- Achievement of any specific goals

Past success does not guarantee future results.

Personal Responsibility

By reading this book, you acknowledge that:

- You are solely responsible for your own choices, decisions, and actions.

- You assume all risks from implementing any strategies or exercises.

- You will seek professional guidance when appropriate.

- You will not hold the author, H2P Collective Corp., the publisher, or distributors liable for any outcomes, positive or negative.

You agree to hold harmless Liz St James, Raphael St James, H2P Collective Corp., the publisher, and all distributors from any claims, damages, or losses arising from your use of this book.

Accuracy and Context

While efforts have been made to ensure accuracy, information may become outdated due to changing laws, research, workplace practices, or societal norms.

This book reflects the author's experiences as a Latina woman in specific contexts (Brooklyn and Southern California, the hospitality industry, the period 2000–2025). Cultural contexts, systemic barriers, and opportunities vary significantly across regions, industries, and circumstances.

Readers are responsible for:

- Verifying current information with authoritative sources

- Adapting frameworks to their unique contexts

- Exercising critical thinking and discernment

Third-Party Resources

Mentions of products, services, organizations, or resources are for informational purposes only and do not constitute endorsements. The author is not responsible for the quality, accuracy, or outcomes of third-party products, services, or resources.

The crisis resources listed (hotlines, etc.) are operated by independent organizations not affiliated with the author or publisher.

Copyright and Permitted Use

All content, including worksheets, frameworks, and the Synovial Space methodology application, is copyrighted by Liz St James.

Personal use permitted: Complete worksheets for your own development; photocopies for personal use only.

Commercial use requires written permission. Use in coaching programs, training, courses, public presentations, or derivative works is prohibited without authorization.

Contact for permission: info@h2pcollective.com

Limitation of Liability

To the fullest extent permitted by law, the author, H2P Collective Corp., the publisher, and all associated parties are not liable for any direct, indirect, incidental, consequential, or punitive damages—including loss of income, emotional distress, physical injury, professional setbacks, financial losses, or any other damages—arising from use of this book.

Total liability shall not exceed the purchase price of this book.

Some jurisdictions do not allow certain liability limitations. If any provision is unenforceable, remaining provisions remain in full effect.

Contact and Updates

For questions, permission requests, or coaching services:

Liz St James, H2P Collective Corp. Email: LStjames@h2pcollective.com Website: www.h2pcollective.com

The most current disclaimer version is available at www.h2pcollective.com.

This disclaimer is governed by the laws of the State of Florida.

ACKNOWLEDGMENT

By continuing to read this book, you acknowledge that you have read, understood, and agree to this disclaimer and all its terms.

If you do not agree, discontinue use immediately and return the book for a refund.

Dedication:

The women who came before me paved the way.
Now is our turn to lead unrestricted.

This book is dedicated to my ancestors, who set the stage for me. They pumped purpose and resilience into my blood. They are the foundation of who I am and who I will be.

To my mother, who taught me that strength is not the absence of struggle but the courage to rise again, and who learned to walk when her body said she couldn't, showing me that limitations are only temporary if we refuse to accept them.

To my father, whose journey through sobriety and commitment to educating himself proves that we can rewrite our stories and break free from any restriction that tries to define us.

To my daughters, who inspire me daily as I watch them face their own limitations with grace and determination, reminding me that this work of leading unrestricted is not just for us but for the generations to follow.

To my sisters, my unwavering support system, who see my potential even when I can't. You never look at me sideways when I come up with new and crazy ideas. You never skip a beat; you just believe. Your faith in me fuels my courage to dream bigger.

To my husband, who constantly reminds me of the light I carry inside when I forget it's there. You give me the support and space to lead unrestricted, and you never let me minimize the impact I've had on others. You see the lives I've touched when I'm too close to notice. Thank you for being my mirror and my anchor.

To all the women and men in my life, each of you has shown me what it means to lead with passion despite the obstacles. You are my village, my strength, my reminder that we rise together.

Foreword by Raphael St James

I was Operations Manager at Planned Companies, managing 120+ frontline staff across numerous luxury Manhattan residential properties, when I had a realization that would fundamentally change how I understand transformation. I'd spent two decades building systems to create movement—in organizations, in teams, in people's bodies. I'd been dealing with early-onset osteoarthritis since childhood, and more recently dealing with severe pain from ossifications growing throughout my body. I understood constraints. I'd led operations at luxury hotels, managed the #1 spa location in JFK Terminal 4, and recruited and developed teams across multiple industries.

But I'd never seen anyone systematize movement across all dimensions of life the way my wife did.

When I met Llz, she was Assistant Director of Housekeeping at a boutique health and wellness hotel where I'd just started as Fitness Concierge. I watched her coordinate complex operations, develop team members, navigate union dynamics, and maintain standards under relentless pressure, all while making it look effortless. What I recognized in her wasn't just competence. It was methodology. She had a system, even if she hadn't formalized it yet.

She'd been living Happy, Healthy, Prosperous for years before we ever gave it a name. While I was systematizing physical movement principles, she was applying those same principles to leadership, relationships, career transitions, and life design. And she was the one who eventually told me something that shifted my entire professional trajectory: "You're not just teaching movement. You're coaching transformation."

She saw what I was doing before I did. Because she'd already been doing it.

We both brought leadership. We both brought structure. We both brought lived wisdom from navigating restrictions in high-pressure environments. What made our partnership powerful was recognizing that we'd each been developing complementary pieces of the same methodology from different angles. I brought systematic assessment and framework development. She brought practical application across circumstances I'd never faced. Together, we created something neither of us could have built alone.

I'll never forget hearing stories of Liz leading a union grievance meeting while six months' pregnant. She was facing a room full of skepticism—some of it gender-based, some of it testing a new leader, all of it legitimate workplace tension that needed navigation. Her General Manager relayed how she'd maintained her composure while being publicly questioned, held space for genuine grievances while protecting operational integrity, and emerged from that meeting having strengthened rather than damaged relationships. That wasn't luck. That wasn't personality. That was the systematic application of principles under extreme constraint.

When I wrote Synovial Space, I drew from decades of experience with chronic pain, operations leadership, and building teams across diverse environments. But I'd never had to handle what Liz has. Managing operations across 600+ guest rooms while facing assumptions about capability based on gender and ethnicity. Sitting in meetings where her authority was questioned simply because of who she was, not what she'd proven. Making a deliberate career transition while co-founding a business, relocating across the country, and maintaining family stability—all simultaneously, all successfully.

Synovial Space provides the framework: the Eight Pillars assessment, the edge expansion protocols, the recovery systems, the architecture of movement. It's a reference manual designed to give you comprehensive tools across all dimensions of life. It stands complete on its own.

Unrestricted shows you what those tools look like under pressure. Not in theory. Not in optimal conditions. In real life, with real restrictions, creating real movement. It also stands complete on its own.

Women don't face single restrictions. They face intersecting, multiplicative restrictions—gender, race, body, societal expectations, family obligations—all compounding simultaneously. I can explain the methodology. Liz demonstrates what it looks like to live it when your Physical pillar is compromised by pregnancy complications, your Professional pillar faces gender-based doubt, your Financial pillar requires you to make a significant transition, and your Relational pillar includes navigating partnership while both of you are transforming, all while maintaining the other four pillars under pressure.

If you want to know whether the Synovial Space methodology works in high-stakes environments with genuine constraints, Unrestricted is the evidence. Every framework, every tool, every piece of guidance in this book comes from restrictions Liz has actually experienced: the union confrontations, the pregnancy complications, the career transition we executed together in September 2025, when we both walked away from our established life in California and relocated to Florida to build the life we'd envisioned together. A life where we could work side by side, honoring our individual skill sets for a unified cause that fulfills our purpose.

You don't need one book to understand the other. But if you engage with both, they create something more powerful: a complete system with both the framework and the lived proof that it works under conditions that test every assumption about what's possible.

My wife is one of the most resilient, strategic, and purposeful leaders I've worked alongside. And I've worked with hundreds. She doesn't just teach about moving through restrictions. She's lived every single principle in these pages while leading teams, raising daughters, opening businesses, and refusing to let others' limitations define her capacity. She's demonstrated repeatedly that the very restrictions that seem most permanent are often the doorways to movement we couldn't have imagined from where we started.

If you're a woman who's been told you can't lead because you're "too young," "too emotional," "too anything," this book will show you how to move through those restrictions without destroying yourself trying to prove people wrong. If you're navigating multiple roles—mother, professional, partner, leader—and feeling like you're failing at all of them, Liz will show you how to create sustainable movement across all pillars simultaneously.

And regardless of gender, this book offers something critical: a view of what the methodology looks like under pressure. The principles apply universally, even as the specific restrictions may differ. What Liz demonstrates is that systematic transformation isn't reserved for people with optimal circumstances. It's most powerful precisely when circumstances are most constrained.

When Liz decided to write this book, I told her the world needed her voice. Not as "the wife of the Synovial Space author" but as Liz St James, the executive who led through impossible circumstances. The mother who coped with physical restrictions while maintaining her career, refusing to let others' limitations define her capacity. The leader who created annual women's leadership events because she recognized that the women coming behind her needed to see what was possible. The leader who created the first "Take your kids to work day" that hotel ever had. The strategist who planned an eight-year career transition while maintaining excellence in her current role because she understood that building a bridge is different from burning one down.

I've watched her live these principles for 20 years. I've seen her create movement where others saw only walls. I've witnessed her transform restrictions into doorways—not occasionally, not accidentally, but systematically, across every dimension of life, under conditions that would have justified staying stuck.

If you're standing at a crossroads where every path looks blocked, you're in the right place. Liz has been there. She knows the way through. Not around restrictions. Not despite them. Through them—transforming walls into doorways, methodically and sustainably, while maintaining your integrity and building the life you actually want to live.

That's what it means to lead unrestricted.

Welcome to the methodology that proves it's possible.

Author's Note

Restriction has a way of finding you when you least expect it—and sometimes in the quiet moments when everything has changed.

I spent over 20 years in hospitality leadership, rising from café attendant to Director of Rooms. I helped manage multi-million-dollar renovations, helped lead union meetings, and became the first female Latina Director of Rooms at a 60-year-old historic golf resort in Southern California. I have opened hotels, trained thousands of associates, and built teams that consistently exceeded industry standards, all while being a wife and mother of two daughters.

However, none of these titles or achievements prepared me for the moment when I found myself sitting in a two-bedroom downtown Tampa apartment, stripped of everything I'd built my identity around, looking in the mirror and asking who I was in this new environment. Without the title, the California home acreage, the career I'd built my identity around, who was I, really?

This is what restriction feels like. It's not always the loud, obvious barriers we expect, but the quiet disorientation of standing in unfamiliar territory, unsure of how to move forward.

Here's what I learned: we don't move *past* our restrictions. We move *within* them. The difference matters. Moving past our restrictions suggests we leave them behind, that we outrun or avoid them. Moving through them means we feel them, face them, and allow them to reshape us into something stronger. It means we don't wait for the restriction to disappear before we lead. Instead, we lead within it, despite it, because of it.

This book is my roadmap for anyone who's ever felt lost in their own reflection.

My husband created what he calls the Synovial Space methodology, which is a framework for understanding how we create room for movement in our lives, just as our joints need proper space to function. I have lived and will continue to live this methodology. Where there's no space, there can be no movement. I had to create internal space before I could move forward.

This isn't your typical self-help workbook promising transformation in three easy steps or prescribing a one-size-fits-all approach to success. This is a guide for women navigating real restrictions, whether they're physical, financial, professional, or deeply personal. Learning to create movement within them, not around them. It's about the resilience that comes from sitting with discomfort long enough to find your authentic path forward, not from someone else's blueprint. It's about self-motivation that doesn't ignore your reality but works with it, transforms through it, and leads despite it.

I started in East New York, Brooklyn, where some days it was safe to sit on the stoop or play outside, and other days you never knew if you'd find yourself in the center of violence. From there, I broke through every barrier people said would define me: graduating early, building an over 20-year career in hospitality, running a successful home daycare, and now standing as co-founder of our businesses, mother, wife, leader, and guide. My journey from Brooklyn to executive leadership to life coach demonstrates what happens when you systemically create space within restrictions across all eight pillars of life.

What I've learned is this: restrictions aren't walls. They're doorways. And on the other side of every limitation I've faced has been a version of myself I didn't know I could become.

If you're standing at a crossroad where every path looks blocked, this book will give you tools to create your own trail.

Read it straight through, or jump to a life pillar that calls to you. You can complete the exercises directly in this book or in a separate journal. You may also choose to share the book with other women. **The biggest thing that I ask of you is to self-reflect, give yourself grace, and pay it forward!**

CHAPTER 1

Gunshots in Brooklyn

Understanding Restriction as a Starting Point

We don't get to choose our restrictions. We can choose what to do with them.

I was five years old when I learned that the world wasn't safe. My big cousin came to pick me up as usual from the school yard of what was formerly known as PS. 72 on Shepherd Avenue in East New York, Brooklyn. The school was just a few short blocks from home. As we were walking, we heard gunshots very close by. We saw people screaming and yelling. My cousin and I ran to the nearest place that we could take cover, which happened to be an empty lot with overgrown grass and weeds. We crouched down as low as possible for hours, until sundown. I was so scared and confused about what was happening and how someone could be doing this. We were there for a while, fearful that if we left too early, we might get caught in the crosshairs of something. We walked home in the dark.

That day in the empty lot taught me my first lesson about restriction: there's always the choice to move through your restrictions. I didn't know then that this understanding would become the foundation of everything I would build.

Sometimes, the first lesson of survival is learning when to stay small so you can live to grow big.

What Is Restriction?

Restriction shapes how you move, not what stops you. It isn't just a challenge, a permanent wall, or a roadblock. It's also not an excuse to diminish your talents or a reason to quit. Restriction is an invitation to create new strategies, and a limit you learn to work with. Restriction is a redirection toward unexpected paths you thought you would never take. Restrictions can be both external and internal.

My Journey Through Professional Restrictions

Before I share the framework for moving through restrictions, let me give you context for how I learned these principles. My career wasn't a straight line. It was a series of restrictions that forced me to get creative.

Early Career (2000–2013): I started as a summer intern, then worked my way up through a hotel company, eventually helping to manage guest services through a multimillion-dollar renovation that expanded a hotel from 526 to 616 rooms. I developed training programs that led to several associate promotions. I learned to navigate through union environments, manage cross-functional teams, and lead through organizational change during hotel acquisitions and rebranding.

Clowning Around (2011–2012): I went to clown school in New York and became Clown Layla for birthday parties and community events part-time.

Daycare and Early Childhood Education (2013–2015): At the peak of my hospitality career, I chose to open a family daycare: a decision that looked like stepping back, but that taught me more about entrepreneurship, financial management, and creative problem-solving than any corporate role could have. After closing the daycare, I explored teaching in a Montessori school for pre-K, then became a second-grade schoolteacher in a charter school for a short stint.

Return to Hospitality (2015–2025): I returned to leadership roles in hospitality, eventually becoming Director of Rooms at a resort in Southern California. The resort was built in 1965, has over 600 guest rooms and villas, sits on over 400 acres of land, and includes two championship golf courses, eight pools, and, currently, the largest meeting space footprint in the Southwest. I trained over 1,000 staff members, helped manage a multimillion-dollar room renovation, managed significant budgets, and created the property's first International Women's History Month event for its leaders.

Life Coaching (2017– present): In self-reflection, I came to the realization that coaching people in my leadership roles was what gave me purpose. I decided to undertake one-on-one life coaching training, and then I started to do pro bono coaching part-time. Now, in 2025, I have started my life coaching business full-time with my husband, Raphael St James, based on his Synovial Space methodology.

Let's talk through a few different types of restrictions.

Environmental/Geographic Restrictions

Living in East New York, Brooklyn had its highs and lows. The highs were being around family, summers hanging around the block with friends, the familiar sound of the Mr. Softee ice cream truck every afternoon, and taking a dollar to the bodega to get a quarter water, bag of chips, ice, and candy! Those were the days. Despite these fond memories, crime was still rampant, but we found ways through those restrictions. I chose to go to a high school outside of my East New York area. The dropout rates at schools in my zone were high, and graduation rates were at an all-time low. I decided to move past this restriction, traveling on two trains and a bus daily and taking one semester of night school to graduate one year early.

While my environment at the time restricted me, it taught me that I could find alternatives. The path that's presented to you isn't the only path you can take.

Throughout my travels, one thing I've noticed is that sometimes, people bring their mentality from where they grew up to anywhere they go in the future. For me, the sense of heightened awareness and safety, and being aware of my surroundings, has always stayed. Where you come from makes you stronger. Whether it's a rural area, working on the land, or the concrete jungle, everyone takes their unique strengths from their environment.

Economic Restrictions

My father migrated from Puerto Rico with his family at a young age. My grandfather was great with his hands and would try to do any possible job to support his household. He did this with only one leg, as he'd unfortunately lost the other leg one day while working the sugar cane fields in Puerto Rico. The money he earned by doing odds-and-ends jobs in the neighborhood was barely enough for rent and food. My father had holes in his sneakers and was ashamed to go to school. He'd rather have worked just like his father did so he could make money to contribute to his family. He learned how to read on his own by reading the local newspapers, taught himself how to write, and eventually was able to get a job in the NYC public school system as a janitor. His economic status prevented him from getting a higher-paying job at the time; however, he was able to retire from that job while owning a home for his family. This taught me that your economic status doesn't define who you are, and that it's possible to carry out your dreams.

Gender/Systemic Restrictions

In my hospitality career, I learned that some of the most limiting restrictions aren't written in policy.

I will never forget one conversation that my mentor had with me. He informed me that the hiring manager for a promotion I was going to apply for wanted to hire a man for the role. The manager's reasoning was both simple and frustrating to me: he felt the role was better suited for a man given the "clientele" of the hotel. I applied anyway. I didn't apply because I wanted to prove him wrong. I applied because I knew I was qualified. I applied because I understood the operation, the team dynamics, and the guest experience. I applied because the manager's restriction (his limited view of who could lead) didn't have to become mine.

I got the position, and I excelled in it. The hiring manager even admitted it, so I'm not just giving myself praise!

Here's the truth about gender-based restrictions: overcoming one doesn't eliminate the pattern. Throughout my career, I've faced variations of this same bias: the surprise when I demonstrated financial acumen, the subtle doubt when I had to make tough personnel decisions, the raised eyebrows when I negotiated firmly. Each time, I had a choice: accept the restriction as truth or treat it as someone else's limitation that I could move through.

What I learned is that gender restrictions, like all systematic barriers, aren't about you. They're about outdated systems trying to maintain familiar patterns. Your job isn't to tear down the entire system by yourself or to exhaust yourself fighting every battle. Your job is to recognize these restrictions for what they are—someone else's belief about what's possible—and then demonstrate a different reality through your competence, your leadership, and your results. I didn't overcome that leader's bias by convincing him he was wrong. I moved through his restriction by refusing to let his limited vision define my capabilities. In doing so, I created a pathway not just for myself but for other women who came after me.

I clearly remember speaking on the phone one time with a guest who was very irate regarding an experience with her stay. She asked my name, and I said, "Liz St James." She came to stay with us a few months later and asked for me by name at the front desk: "Can I please see Liz St James. I spoke with her on the phone regarding last time I was here."

When I came out to the desk, she gasped very dramatically and said, "Hmmm... I did not picture you to be Liz St James." I knew exactly what she was trying to say. Maybe if I'd had a very Hispanic last name, she would have pictured me to be a young Hispanic woman, or maybe if I'd had a Latin accent, she would have expected someone different. This is the very reason my husband changed his last name as a young man: to get better opportunities than would be possible with his father's last name of Torres, and to not hold the last name of a man who was barely in his life.

That gasp, and the unspoken "You're not what I expected," revealed something I'd been dealing with my entire career. It wasn't just about my gender. It was about how my appearance, my name, and my accent (or lack thereof) shaped how people perceived my competence before I'd said a word.

I'd made choices about this. Straightening my hair in early leadership roles. Keeping my jewelry and accessories small and subtle. I found myself sometimes dimming my light for others to shine more brightly.

These weren't small choices; they were calculations about which version of myself would be taken seriously. And they worked, strategically. But they also cost something.

The guest's gasp revealed the gap between the "Liz St James" she'd imagined and the actual woman standing in front of her. In that moment, I had a choice: to feel diminished by her surprise or to recognize it as information. She'd made an assumption based on my name. That wasn't my problem to solve by becoming what she expected, but it was information about how the world sometimes reads identity.

What identity markers (name, appearance, accent, presentation) do you modify in professional contexts? Why?

What assumptions do people make about you before they meet you?

How does that affect your first interactions?

Where are you "performing" a version of yourself to fit expectations?

What does that cost?

How might reclaiming aspects of your identity strengthen your authority rather than weaken it?

Physical Restrictions

Raphael and I met at work in 2005. We both knew that one of us needed to leave the company to progress in our relationship, and I made the choice to move on after several years there. After my last day, Raphael proposed to me at the top of the Empire State Building. He said that from up there, we could see everywhere we'd been but also where we're headed, and that every time we saw the Empire State Building, whether from a vantage point in the city, in pictures, or in movies, we'd know our history is etched on that rooftop. I said yes, of course.

A few short months into my new job, I was involved in a car accident that changed everything. The inflammation was so severe I couldn't put on a bra. I couldn't lift my daughter (from a previous relationship however, in Raphael's life since she was one and a half). I couldn't work. Physical therapy three times a week became my new routine, with no clear timeline for when I would be released back to work.

Then came the termination phone call. No warning. No accommodation. Just... "You're done; mail us back the work phone."

Unable to work, barely able to care for my daughter, with the wedding months away, and now without my income, I faced what felt like an impossible situation. This wasn't simply a physical restriction; it was physical, financial, and emotional restrictions compounding on each other.

Here's what I learned about restrictions in that moment: they reveal what matters and what doesn't. They show you who you are when everything else is stripped away.

My body needed time to heal, so I gave it that time. I received a call from my previous employer to come back in a new role when I was ready. My sense of justice demanded action, so I decided to file a complaint with the Commission of Human Rights office. This wasn't to retaliate against the company but because I didn't want my experience to happen to another person facing temporary disability. Was the expectation that I wasn't going to fight in some way regarding the injustice? If so, why was that the expectation?

Moving through this restriction didn't mean the injury never happened or that the termination didn't sting. It meant I refused to let those circumstances define my future. I healed, I fought back where it mattered, and I moved forward, not despite the restriction but having learned from it. Eventually, I wound up getting married on the date we'd originally set in August 2007. I flourished in my new job, and the company settled on the complaint.

They gave me compensation for their decision, which we were able to use as downpayment for our first home.

"You may encounter many defeats, but you must not be defeated."
Maya Angelou

The Three Choices When Faced with Re-strictions

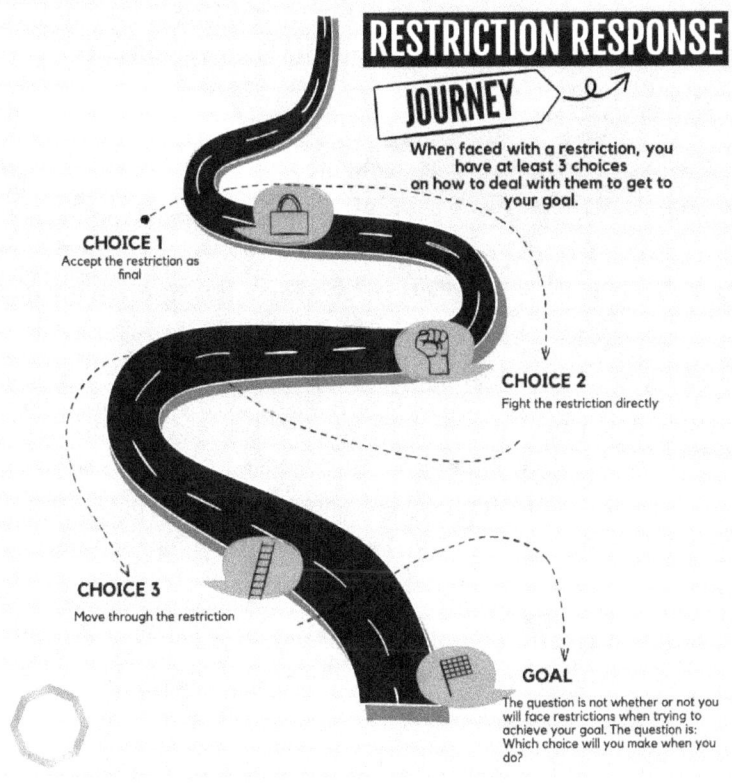

RESTRICTION RESPONSE JOURNEY

When faced with a restriction, you have at least 3 choices on how to deal with them to get to your goal.

CHOICE 1
Accept the restriction as final

CHOICE 2
Fight the restriction directly

CHOICE 3
Move through the restriction

GOAL
The question is not whether or not you will face restrictions when trying to achieve your goal. The question is: Which choice will you make when you do?

When restriction blocks our path, we face three choices. Each one comes with its own cost and consequence.

Choice 1: Accept It as Final

After my youngest daughter reached school age in 2014, I closed my home daycare, sold the house, downsized into a one-bedroom apartment, and eventually, after dipping my toes into teaching, returned to hospitality. I took a demotion to do so, as my new boss was my mentor whom I'd previously worked with, and it was a new company, which allowed me to explore opportunities. My family and I traveled to several hotels within the company, searching for our next chapter. We were looking for a place where we could transfer together and build a new life.

Then we visited California...

A friend working in LA had mentioned a property in Carlsbad, California. I'd never heard of the place, but we decided to visit. From the moment we stepped foot on the property, I fell in love. It was everything I'd envisioned. The location, the views, the opportunity were all there. This was it!

I went online and found a position that fit perfectly. That same day, believe it or not, we set up a tour with an apartment complex, explored the neighborhood, and checked out the closest high school and elementary school for our daughters. I applied for the position immediately. When we returned from vacation, I learned it had already been offered to someone else.

I almost gave up. Right there. I didn't look for another role. I didn't want to explore other hotels. I almost said, "Forget it. We'll just stay where we are in New York."

This is what accepting restriction as final looks like. It's the moment when disappointment convinces us that one closed door means all doors are closed. It's when we let a single "no" become our final answer.

The Cost of Acceptance

When we accept restrictions as final, we pay in the possibilities never explored. We pay in the person we never become. We pay in the life we never build.

If I'd stopped there, my family would have missed seven years in Southern California. I would have missed career growth, the resort experience, and the promotions that came from that iconic golf resort. We would never have purchased our home in the Vista hilltops. My daughters would never have experienced that different SoCal environment. And I would have spent years wondering, "What if...?"

The cost of accepting restriction as final isn't just what we lose in that moment. It's also the compounding effect of all the moments that never happen because we stopped moving.

Choice 2: Fight It Directly

Fighting the restriction head-on means confronting the barrier with force. This means demanding reconsideration, challenging the decision, and insisting on what we believe we deserve. Sometimes, it's necessary. However, fighting directly can also drain energy, create conflict, and close doors permanently if not done strategically.

In the Carlsbad situation, I could have called the hiring manager and insisted they reconsider since I was an internal candidate. I could have fought for that specific role. But direct confrontation wasn't the right path here. The position had already been offered, and fighting that decision would have positioned me as being difficult even before I started.

The Cost of Fighting Directly

Fighting every restriction head-on exhausts you. It can burn bridges and create a reputation you don't want, and it can sometimes win you battles while losing the war. There's a time to fight directly, but it's not every time. You must weigh your options each time you're faced with a restriction to see if it's a good decision to fight it head-on.

Choice 3: Move Through It

Moving through restriction means staying alert to alternative paths, remaining open to different routes to the same destination, and trusting that one closed door doesn't mean the whole building is locked.

I didn't give up on Carlsbad. I immediately reached out to my Director of HR and made my intentions crystal clear: "If anything changes, please let me know. I'm very interested in this property."

That simple act of staying visible, staying interested, and making my commitment known changed everything. About a week later, I got the call. The person who'd been offered the position had declined it. They asked if I could task force at the property. I said yes without hesitation. I showed up, did excellent work, and earned the position.

We moved to Carlsbad. I stayed for seven years. I was promoted. We purchased our home in the Vista hilltops of Southern California. Everything I'd envisioned that first day on the property became reality. I didn't force it, and I didn't give up, but I moved through the restriction.

The Power of Moving Through

Moving through restrictions requires patience, adaptability, and strategic persistence. It means clearly communicating your intentions without demanding immediate results. It means staying ready, staying excellent, and positioning yourself for opportunities when they arise. It means understanding that the timing might not be yours to control, but your response is.

Notice what moving through looks like in practice: I didn't fight for the position because it was already offered to someone else. I didn't accept defeat and stop trying. Instead, I made my interest known, stayed ready, and, when the opportunity shifted, I was positioned to step in.

Everyone has their own personal beliefs. My personal belief is that everything happens for a reason and what is meant for me will be for me.

The question isn't whether you will face restrictions. You WILL face them. The question is: which choice will you make when you do?

Your past doesn't have to predict your future. Your restrictions don't have to define your possibilities.

Different Restrictions We Face: The Reality We Navigate

Restrictions in the Workplace

Remember that hiring manager I mentioned earlier in the chapter, who said he wanted a man for the leadership position I wished to apply for? That moment wasn't an isolated incident. It was a window into a pattern that women experience throughout their careers.

The restrictions women often face aren't written in policy manuals. They live in assumptions about who should lead, who can handle pressure, and who belongs in certain roles. I've seen this play out repeatedly in my own career and those of friends and family members.

The data tells a clear story, but women live it daily. We work harder to be seen as equally competent. We have to find our way through the double bind of being neither too soft nor too aggressive, neither too collaborative nor not decisive enough. We cry or show our feelings in the workplace, are seen as too emotional, and get questioned about whether we're the right fit for our leadership role. We see male colleagues advance on potential while women advance on proof. That proof often requires more hours, more projects, and more evidence of capability before we're deemed ready for the next level.

These workplace restrictions can come with tangible costs:

- Income sacrifice: Taking longer to reach the same positions means years of lower earnings, which compounds over a career and affects retirement, wealth-building, and financial security.

- Time sacrifice: Working harder to prove competence means less time for family, personal development, or rest. The "second shift" at home combined with the "extra shift" to prove workplace worth creates unsustainable pressure.

- Opportunity cost: Energy spent navigating bias is energy not spent on innovation, creativity, or strategic thinking.

We lose what we might have created if we weren't constantly managing perceptions.

Personally, I would constantly second-guess how I was being perceived since I was not only female but also Latina. I was given the stigma of being rude, too abrupt, and too fast from fellow Latinos. In most leadership roles I stepped into, I would get judged by what I looked like, not by who I was as a person or as a leader. I clearly remember starting off in one of my roles and making sure not to wear my curly hair out. I felt that if I wanted to be taken seriously, I needed to give in to what was then the societal norm, brush my hair back, and tie it up. Please don't get me wrong: I understand that times are changing and evolving. However, I can guarantee for sure that at some point, one or two or many of you reading this will have experienced gender bias in the workplace. If you haven't, phenomenal! If you have or are currently, here are some tips on how to move through the gender-based restrictions.

Here's what I learned: You don't overcome systemic restrictions by waiting for the system to change completely, and you don't need to exhaust yourself by fighting every instance of bias. You move through by understanding two fundamental principles: integrity vs. approval, and self-confidence as a strategy.

Integrity vs. Approval

When that hiring manager doubted whether a woman could handle the role, I didn't try to convince him. I didn't argue my case or defend my gender capability. I applied anyway. I let my qualifications speak. I moved with integrity. I stayed true to my competence, my experience, and my value regardless of his limitations.

Integrity means:

- Knowing your worth independent of others' recognition
- Making decisions based on your capabilities, not others' doubts
- Refusing to shrink to fit others' expectations
- Demonstrating excellence without apology

Self-Confidence as a Strategy

Self-confidence in the face of gender bias isn't about being louder or more aggressive. It's about internal certainty that external doubt cannot shake. When I excelled in that leadership role, it wasn't because I was proving him wrong. It was because I'd never accepted his doubt as truth about me in the first place.

This kind of confidence is strategic:

- It conserves your energy for performance, not persuasion.
- It positions you for opportunities when they arise.
- It creates a track record that speaks louder than bias.
- It models possibility for other women watching your path.

The Reality of Moving Through

Moving through gender-based restrictions doesn't mean pretending they don't exist or that they don't affect you. It means refusing to let them define your ceiling. It means understanding that their limitation is not your limitation.

When you move through with integrity and self-confidence, you do more than advance your own career. You create cracks in the system for those coming behind you. Every woman who excels in a role someone said she couldn't handle makes it slightly easier for the next woman to be considered.

Beyond Gender

These same restrictions and these same strategies for moving through them apply to other forms of workplace bias as well. I've witnessed colleagues face doubt and prejudice because of their sexual orientation, their age, their background, or other aspects of their identity that had nothing to do with their capability to do the job.

I've watched people move through these restrictions with the same principles: integrity that wouldn't compromise and self-confidence that external doubt couldn't shake. They didn't wait for perfect acceptance. They didn't exhaust themselves justifying their right to be there. They showed up, performed excellently, and let their results rewrite the narrative.

The bias was real. The restrictions existed. However, so did their competence and their choice in how they responded.

Whether the restriction comes from assumptions about your gender, your sexual orientation, or any other part of your identity, the path through remains the same:

- **Know your worth.**
- **Demonstrate your excellence.**
- **Refuse to accept someone else's limited vision as the boundary of your potential.**

The restrictions are real. The bias exists, but so do your capability, your competence, and your choice in how you respond.

Restrictions in Leadership

Sometimes, the harshest restrictions come from unexpected sources. You expect bias from certain quarters, but when it comes from someone who should understand your struggle, it cuts differently.

I walked into a grievance meeting early in my time managing a complex union property. One of the union's key leaders, a woman herself, looked at me as I entered the room full of male leaders and made it immediately clear that she thought I was too young and inexperienced to be in this role. Her comments, delivered loud enough for everyone to hear, dismissed my capability before I'd even sat down.

I smiled, kept my composure, and proceeded with the meeting. I wouldn't let her comments and her external thought process intimidate me.

As we worked through the grievance, I quoted specific portions of the collective bargaining agreement (CBA) and their interpretations. These were details she didn't know I was aware of. I calmly reminded her that this was not my first rodeo. I'd been working in union hotels as a leader for many years; I was no novice. I wasn't claiming to be an expert either, but I was knowledgeable and confident in my understanding of the CBA and my leadership responsibilities.

By the end of that meeting, the energy had shifted. She respected me. Years later, we developed a cordial relationship built on mutual understanding of our goals for the team.

The Real Issue

Here's what the moment taught me. The complaints she was receiving weren't because I didn't know how to lead. They came from team members who weren't following the CBA, and I was holding them accountable. The restriction was not my ability to lead. It was their shock that I knew what I was doing and wouldn't back down from enforcing standards.

That union leader expected to walk in and intimidate a woman who was in over her head. Instead, she found a leader who'd done her homework, knew her stuff, and wouldn't be shaken down by public humiliation tactics.

Moving Through Leadership Restrictions

My leadership has been questioned many times throughout my career. The restrictions show up as doubt, as dismissiveness, as surprise that I know what I'm talking about.

Each time, I move through the same way:

- **Inform yourself:** Learn what you don't know. Study the systems, policies, and frameworks that govern your work. Knowledge is armor against assumptions about your capability.

- **Be knowledgeable:** It's not enough to learn once. Stay current, understand nuances, and know your material cold. When someone questions you, your depth of understanding speaks louder than their doubt.

- **Lead with self-confidence:** Not arrogance, not defensiveness, but the quiet confidence that comes from competence. When that union leader tried to undermine me publicly, my calm response and demonstrated knowledge did more than any defensive reaction could have.

The restriction was never about my actual ability to lead. It was about their assumption that someone who looked like me couldn't possibly know what she was doing. Moving through meant proving nothing. It just meant being fully prepared, fully knowledgeable, and fully confident in what I brought to the table.

With every limitation, there is a choice.

Restrictions in Body

A few short months after Raphael and I got married in 2007; we got pregnant with our first child together. At our four-month ultrasound check-up, we were excited to add to our family. The ultrasound technician looked at the screen, then turned it away from us. "I'll be right back with the doctor," she said.

The doctor informed us that the baby no longer had a heartbeat. I would need to schedule a D&C to remove the baby.

Our world fell apart at that moment.

I called my dad as we left the office. He'd been so excited for us, and he couldn't wait to meet his new grandchild. When I told him the news, he cried hysterically on the phone. I didn't understand it fully then, but I realize now that he must have known this would have been the last grandchild he would physically meet.

When Your Body Becomes the Restriction

In that moment, my body was my restriction. The societal expectation is clear: get married, grow your family, live happily ever after. We'd just moved into our first apartment together. Everything was progressing according to plan. Except my body had other plans.

The Hidden Costs

The emotional toll was devastating. We leaned on each other, but the grief was profound and isolating in ways I hadn't anticipated.

The career impact was unexpected. My employer knew I was pregnant. My belly was starting to show. Close family and friends knew. Having to tell them about the loss made it worse. Each conversation reopened the wound. Each sympathetic look at work reminded me of what we'd lost.

Moving Through Physical Restriction

Moving through this restriction required accepting that some things are beyond our control while focusing intensely on what we could control. I made sure to take care of my health and my body so we could try again. If I were to be a vessel for our child, it was important for me to love myself and take care of myself, especially since I have hypertension.

I also held on to my belief that everything happens for a reason. There was some reason that child didn't come into this world. I wasn't sure what the reason was at the time, and maybe I'll never know. Holding space for the possibility that there was a meaning even in this loss helped me move forward without becoming bitter or defeated.

Physical restrictions are perhaps the hardest to move through because they feel so absolute. Your body doesn't negotiate. It doesn't respond to willpower or determination alone. But even within these restrictions, movement is possible in how we care for ourselves, in how we process grief, and in how we prepare for what comes next.

"Courage is like a muscle. We strengthen it by use." Ruth Gordon

Restrictions in Caregiving:

Every night, when my oldest daughter was younger, I would read her a bedtime story. She slept on the top area of a loft bed that had a desk, shelves, and a play area below. I would climb the stairs and read while lying next to her.

She was about eight years old when everything changed.

A few minutes into the story one night, she started to fall asleep. Then her body began shaking. I watched for a few seconds, thinking it was a night terror. I tried to wake her up. It happened repeatedly. These weren't night terrors; they were seizures. I called 911 immediately. The neurologist diagnosed her with a rare form of epilepsy called benign rolandic epilepsy. He prescribed daily medication and gave me an emergency injection to administer if a seizure lasted beyond a certain time. Then he told me something that made my heart sink: there was a possibility that the seizures and medications could cause cognitive slowing. He tried to reassure me that this type of epilepsy usually resolves in adolescence, but all I could think about was protecting my daughter.

The Restriction of Caregiving

As a caregiver, my restriction became clear. I couldn't prevent the seizures. I couldn't control when they would happen or how severe they would be. My daughter's body had become unpredictable, and my role was to be vigilant, prepared, and present.

Every night, I lay with her past those critical first 10 minutes of sleep, watching, waiting, ready. One night, she had a very long seizure and started foaming at the mouth. I called 911. Then called again because they weren't coming fast enough. Time stopped. I was terrified she wouldn't come out of it, terrified of brain damage, terrified of cognitive decline.

When the paramedics finally arrived, she came out of the seizure. The tests came back clear at the hospital, but the fear remained.

The Hidden Costs

The restriction of caregiving extracted costs I hadn't anticipated:

- Sleep and rest: Years of watching her for those first 10 minutes every night, never fully relaxing until I knew she was safe. I knew as a parent that sleepless nights were a part of what I'd signed up for, but this was a different type of restlessness.

- Career limitations: Needing flexibility for neurologist appointments if required.

- Emotional toll: The constant vigilance, the fear that never fully goes away, the helplessness of watching your child suffer.

- Lost spontaneity: Every decision for sleepovers with friends or going over to a family member's house was filtered through "What if she has a seizure?"

Moving Through Caregiving Restrictions

I couldn't eliminate the restriction, but I could move through it by becoming an expert on my daughter's condition. I read everything I could find about benign rolandic epilepsy. I researched treatment options, triggers, outcomes. I learned how to properly handle someone having a seizure. More importantly, I started logging everything. How many minutes after falling asleep did the seizure occur? How many nights per week? How long did the seizure last? What did she do today? What did she eat? Was there a pattern? Could I identify triggers?

This documentation became my way of creating control within the uncontrollable. I couldn't stop the seizures, but I could understand them. I could be prepared. I could give the neurologist detailed data that helped inform my daughter's care.

We continued this regimen of neurologist checkups, daily medication, and nightly monitoring until she was 13 years old. Then, just as the doctor had predicted, the epilepsy resolved. Thankfully, my daughter didn't lose much cognitive abilities. The opposite, in fact: she graduated a year early from high school and is now headed on a career path to be a dermatologist, because her medical experiences as a child sparked her interest in being a doctor.

The Movement in Caregiving

Moving through caregiving restrictions means accepting that you cannot fix everything while refusing to accept helplessness. It means:

- Informing yourself: Becoming knowledgeable about the condition, the treatments, the possibilities

- Creating systems: Logging, tracking, documenting, turning chaos into data

- Being present: Showing up at every appointment and every moment you're needed

- Maintaining hope: Believing in the possibility of resolution while preparing for the reality of the present

Caregiving restrictions are unique because they're not about you. They're about someone you love. You can't walk away. You can't choose a different path. But you can choose how you show up. You can choose to be informed, prepared, and present. You can choose to move through the restriction with both fierce love and strategic action.

These restrictions aren't excuses. They're context. And understanding the context is the first step toward movement.

"Your limitations aren't obstacles to overcome but invitations to discover new forms of movement that are uniquely available to you. The spaces that seem most restrictive often contain the seeds of your most profound gifts." Raphael St James

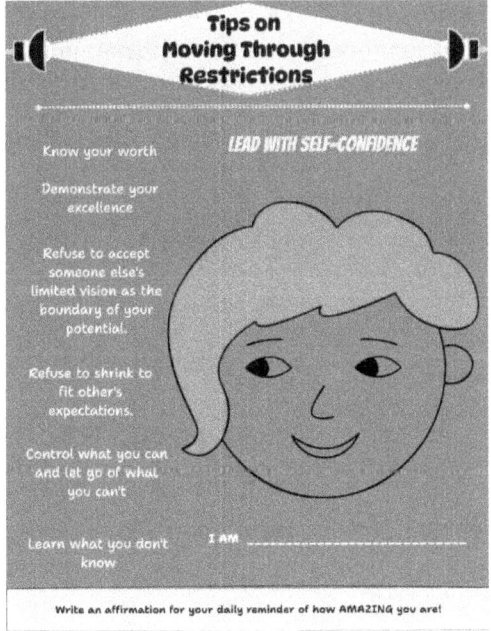

From Restrictions to Transformation: The H2P Collective Story

In 2017, during life coach training, my coach asked me a simple question: "In three words, how do you want to fully live?"

I didn't hesitate: "Happy, healthy, and prosperous."

Those three words captured everything I'd been learning through decades of navigating restrictions. Every barrier I'd faced—gender bias in leadership, financial constraints when opening the daycare, physical limitations during pregnancy, the grief of losing my father—had taught me something about creating sustainable movement through limitations.

H2P Collective was born from that movement. My husband Raphael, with his Synovial Space methodology born from living with osteoarthritis, combined his experiences into a framework for transformation. His physical journey through chronic pain mirrored my professional and personal journey through systemic and circumstantial restrictions.

Together, we co-founded H2P Collective to help others achieve those three goals:

- Happy: Find emotional and relational freedom within constraints

- Healthy: Develop physical and mental resilience despite limitations

- Prosperous: Create financial and professional sustainability aligned with purpose.

This workbook is the culmination of that work. It's the framework we use with clients, the lessons from our career managing complex operations and developing leaders, and the lived experience of moving through restrictions across all eight life pillars.

The methodology works because it's not theory. It's been tested through:

- Leading staff members over multiple departments

- Managing multimillion-dollar projects in union environments

- Opening and running a successful small business

- Navigating physical, financial, and emotional crises

- Rising to pave the way as the first Latina leader in several roles throughout my career

- Co-founding a transformation business that helps others create their own paths through limitations

You're not just reading a book. You're accessing a methodology born from real restrictions, tested in high-pressure environments, and proven to create sustainable movement across all dimensions of life. While this workbook is deeply rooted in my personal Latina/New York/California experience, please note that this perspective will help readers from different backgrounds understand how the framework might apply to their own cultural contexts.

A Preview of the Journey

Just as my husband learned that joints need space in multiple dimensions to move freely, I've learned that leading through limitations requires understanding how restrictions show up across every area of life. The following eight pillars provide a framework from the Synovial Space methodology for recognizing where you face restrictions and how to create movement within them. Each pillar represents a dimension where restrictions appear and where you can learn to lead unrestricted.

Physical pillar: How we relate to our bodies and their limitations

Mental pillar: Creating room for new thoughts when circumstances feel constraining

Emotional pillar: Developing the right balance between connection and independence

Spiritual pillar: Finding purpose, not despite limitations but through them

Professional pillar: Building a career that balances stability and flexibility

Relational pillar: Creating relationships that enable growth without losing connection

Financial pillar: Developing sustainable resource patterns that support your purpose

Purpose pillar: Allowing your unique contribution to emerge and express itself

In the chapters ahead, we'll explore each of these pillars in depth, not as theory but as lived experience. Every story is true.

Every lesson learned and every framework I share with you came from finding my own way through restrictions. The goal is to help you identify your own restrictions and create movement within them. You'll learn not just what to do but how to think differently about the limitations you face.

Why Does Assessing Your Restrictions Matter?

Most of us don't see our restrictions clearly. We either:

1. **Minimize them:** "That's not a big deal." "That's not important now."

2. **Dramatize them:** "This is horrible." "I can't get over this."

3. **Normalize them:** "Everything's fine."

What Clear Assessment Enables

- Early intervention

- Strategic response

- Resource allocation

- Movement instead of emergency management

One important thing to note: even though these are eight distinct life pillars, they are all interconnected. One affects the other, as in the "wheel of life." Movement in one will affect another one or even several others. You're not looking for your wheel to turn on all sides easily; you're just looking for some self-reflection and tools on how you can try and move a little more smoothly through life's restrictions.

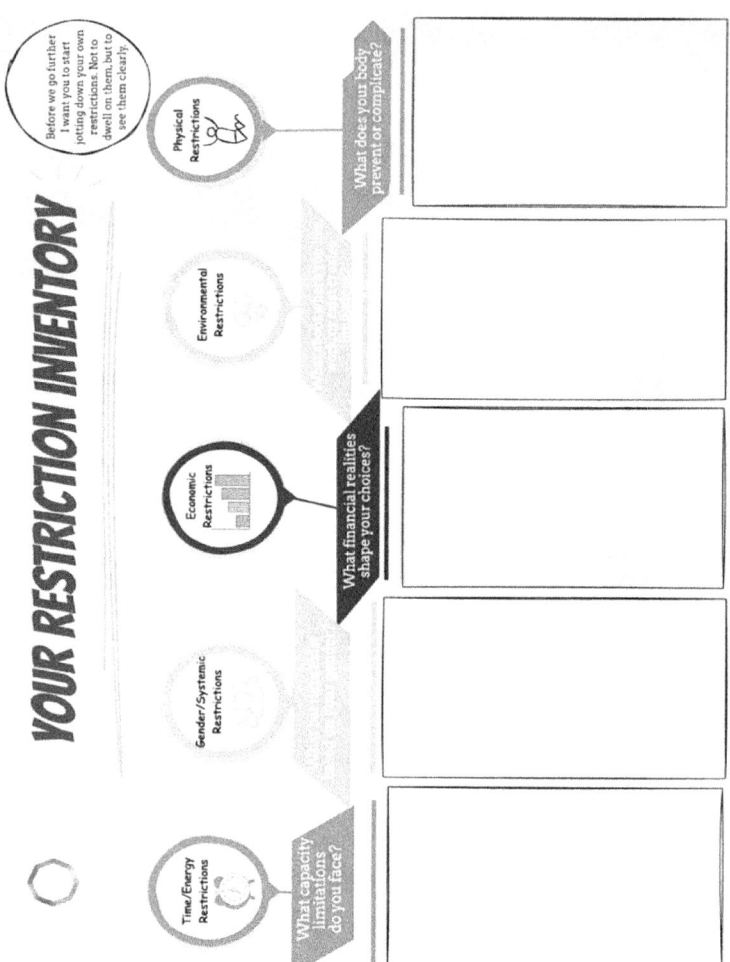

YOUR RESTRICTION INVENTORY

Before we go further I want you to start jotting down your own restrictions. Not to dwell on them, but to see them clearly.

Physical Restrictions

What does your body prevent or complicate?

Environmental Restrictions

Economic Restrictions

What financial realities shape your choices?

Gender/Systemic Restrictions

Time/Energy Restrictions

What capacity limitations do you face?

CHAPTER 2

The Synovial Space Principle

A Framework for Moving Through Restrictions

I was about 19 years old, and I was working at a French bakery café in the Grand Central Station area of NYC while I was in college. This was the best experience as a café attendant because at the end of the night, all the pastries and breads that hadn't been purchased that day would be given to the staff for free or donated to shelters around NYC. I was able to work my way up to a shift supervisor. Every day, there was a customer who would come into my cashier line for lunch. He worked at the men's clothing store across the street, Brooks Brothers. He was always so friendly. We chatted all the time. One day, he asked me what I was studying in college. I told him I was studying business management, but I really wanted to explore hotel or restaurant management. He gave me a contact at a boutique hotel company that owned a few hotels in NYC, saying that they had paid internships and he thought I would be great for one of those positions. He told me to name-drop, as he'd worked there for many years in the past. So, I did... and I was able to get an internship in my first 242 all-suite boutique NYC hotel. I loved every minute of it, and I was getting paid more than my bakery café supervisor job just being a summer intern. That internship turned into an over 20-year career.

The Lesson: I didn't know it then, but this was my first conscious experience with the principle we now call Synovial Space. Just as synovial fluid creates space between bones to enable movement, that daily interaction with a Brooks Brothers employee created space between my current reality (shift supervisor) and my future possibility (hospitality career).

I wasn't stuck at the café. I was positioned there. The restriction of not yet being in the hotel industry wasn't a wall. It was the exact environment where the right connection could form. Like a joint that needs proper alignment before movement can occur, I needed to be in that specific place, serving that specific customer, having built that specific relationship, for the pathway to open.

This is how Synovial Space works in real life. Although we can sometimes create space for movement by forcing doors open (this is option 2 when faced with restriction!), we can also do so by being fully present where we are, building authentic connections, and preparing ourselves internally so that when external opportunities appear, we have the capacity to move through them.

What Is Synovial Space?

The Metaphor: Two Paths to the Same Discovery

My husband Raphael discovered this principle through his own body. At the age of seven, he started to live with osteoarthritis in his hips and sacrum area, which then progressed to stage 2 and stage 3 osteoarthritis. While most people experience joint pain as a limitation that stops movement, Raphael became fascinated by what made movement possible at all. He learned that in a healthy joint, synovial fluid creates and maintains space between the bones. This space is what allows movement to occur. Without adequate space, bone grinds on bone. With proper space, even compromised joints can move.

His osteoarthritis taught him something counterintuitive. The restriction itself revealed how movement works. By understanding what was breaking down his joints, he discovered the principle of how space enables all movement. His physical limitations became his greatest teacher about the mechanics of mobility.

I discovered this principle differently. Through years of navigating barriers in my career, relationships, and personal life, I learned that where there's restriction, you can move through it. I began connecting this insight to the restrictions I was currently facing, and, looking back, I recognized how I'd moved through numerous restrictions in my past without even naming what I was doing.

This was an epiphany for me. What Raphael discovered through the biology of his joints was something I'd learned through life coaching training and leadership experience. We'd arrived at the same truth from completely different directions: one through the physical body and lived experiences, and one through lived experiences alone.

The Biology

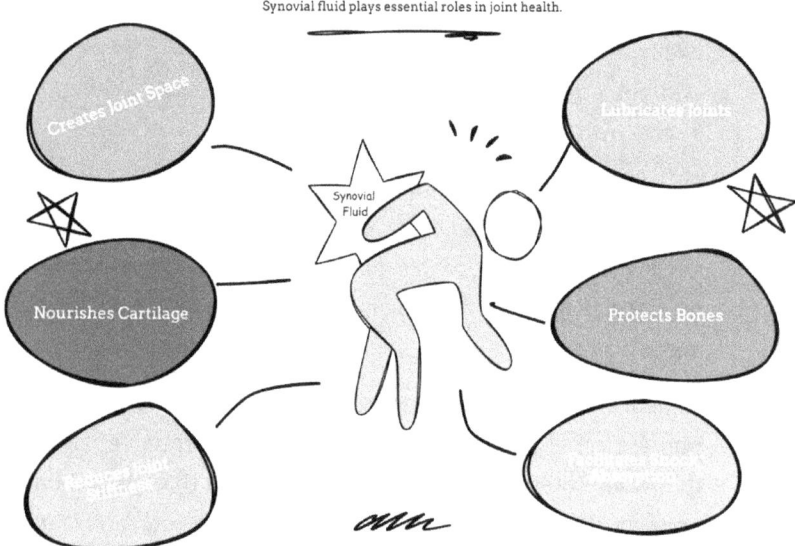

Without the right synovial space, movement becomes painful, restricted, and eventually impossible. The joint needs this space. It needs this gap between the bones to function. The space is not empty or wasted. It is the essential condition that makes movement possible.

The Life Application: How Constraints Create Structure for Movement

Just as synovial fluid creates space within the structure of a joint, life's constraints create a structure so you can move meaningfully.

This is the principle of Synovial Space applied to life:

Where there appears to be a restriction, there is the potential for movement—if we understand how to create and use the space within those constraints.

Think about it: a kite soars highest not when the string is cut and it's "free" but when there's tension on the string. The string is the restriction. It's what allows the kite to catch the wind and rise. Without that constraint pulling against it, the kite would simply fall.

Similarly, our restrictions, whether physical, financial, professional, or relational, aren't just obstacles. They're the string that creates the tension necessary for us to soar.

My Understanding: Moving Through Not Past

Here's the key insight that changed everything for me:

Movement doesn't happen *despite* restriction. Movement happens *through* restriction.

For years, I thought success meant eliminating barriers and reaching a place where restrictions no longer existed. That's not how growth works, though. Not in our joints, and not in our lives.

The restriction itself creates the conditions that make meaningful movement possible. Just as synovial space exists within the structure of a joint, our capacity for growth exists within the structure of our limitations.

When I couldn't get that position the first time I applied in the Carlsbad resort, the restriction didn't stop my movement. It shaped it. The constraint forced me to stay alert, stay connected, stay ready. When the opportunity shifted, I was positioned to move through it.

The Principle in Practice

Synovial Space, as a life principle, means:

- Recognizing that restrictions aren't walls but frameworks for growth

- Accepting that sustainable growth happens through progressive movement within restrictions, not by eliminating all barriers.

In the sections that follow, we'll explore how this principle applies across all eight dimensions of life: Physical, Mental, Emotional, Spiritual, Professional, Relational, Financial, and Purpose. You'll learn not just to accept restrictions but to use them as the very structure that enables your most meaningful movement forward.

"She was unstoppable, not because she did not have failures or doubts, but because she continued on despite them." Beau Taplin

CHAPTER 3:

The Physical Pillar

PHYSICAL PILLAR: When your body sets the boundaries

After I miscarried the first time, I grieved, I healed, and, when I was ready, we tried again. I got pregnant. The whole pregnancy, I was so nervous. I was hoping this time would be different.

At my six-month mark, everything changed. My blood pressure spiked. I was already dilating, and it was way too early. The doctor was very clear with me: I needed to be on complete bed rest. Hypertension could turn into preeclampsia. My body was giving me a warning I couldn't ignore.

I spent the summer at home, trying my best to stay in bed, to nurture my body (despite the crazy pizza, cheeseburger, and

Häagen-Dazs cravings), and to do everything right. Every day felt like a negotiation between what I wanted (to be active, to prepare, to play with my oldest daughter) and what my body demanded (stillness, rest, surrender).

"Sometimes the bravest thing you can do is rest." Brené Brown (paraphrased)

I made it to full-term, but even then, my body wasn't cooperating with anyone else's timeline. The doctor induced labor because my hypertension was still a threat to me, to the baby, and to everything we'd worked so hard to protect.

I finally gave birth, but immediately afterward, my blood pressure skyrocketed to dangerous levels. I was rushed to the ICU. They pumped medicine through my veins to bring the pressure down. For days, I was hospitalized, unable to hold my newborn daughter, as much as I desperately wanted to. Raphael learned very quickly how to master the perfect swaddle. When I was finally discharged, I felt disconnected from my own body. I was high on medications, exhausted from the battle, and grieving the birth experience I'd hoped for.

Then came the doctor's final restriction: "You should not have another child. If we hadn't been able to control your blood pressure, you'd have had a stroke. You could have died." My body had drawn a line I couldn't cross.

As a woman, my body's restrictions during pregnancy carried added weight. Society sometimes expects women to "bounce back," to make pregnancy and childbirth look effortless, to minimize our physical struggles so others stay comfortable. The pressure as a woman was to take care of all things, to downplay my hypertension, to keep working, to not "complain" about bed rest.

Learning to advocate for my body, to take my physical boundaries seriously despite others' discomfort—that was leading unrestricted.

The Lesson: Physical restrictions aren't just about what your body can't do. They're about what your body is telling you about boundaries, capacity, and the need for different kinds of strength.

During that pregnancy, I learned three critical lessons about physical space:

1) **Recognizing when your body is setting boundaries vs. when it needs support to push through**

There's a crucial difference between discomfort that signals growth and warning signs that demand you stop.

Early in my bed rest days, I kept trying to push through—doing small tasks, staying active in ways that I thought were harmless—but I felt my body was being dramatic or weak. In reality, it was setting a boundary for survival. Learning to distinguish between "this is hard, but I can do it" and "my body is telling me to stop" became essential.

How to recognize the difference:

Boundaries come with escalating warning signs (in my case, the fact that my blood pressure kept rising, and the early dilation). You feel like your body is working against you no matter what you do.

Growth challenges allow you to stabilize yourself with appropriate support.

Growth edges feel hard, but your body responds positively to effort.

Ask yourself: Is my body adapting and strengthening with support, or is it giving me increasingly urgent signals to stop?

2) The movement: working with physical limitations rather than against them

I couldn't tell my blood pressure to behave, even though I wanted to! I couldn't force my body to cooperate with my timeline. What I could do was work with the restrictions my body was setting.

This meant:

- Accepting the doctor's orders instead of resenting them
- Following medication protocols rather than trying to prove I didn't need them
- Asking for help instead of trying to maintain my previous level of independence
- Adjusting my expectations (THIS IS A HUGE ONE!)

Working with your body means accepting its current reality while doing everything you can to support its best function within those limits.

3) Ways to maintain structure when your body feels like the restriction

The hardest part wasn't the physical limitations themselves; it was the loss of control. My body was making decisions for me. My autonomy felt completely stripped away. However, I learned that even when your body sets strict boundaries, you still have choices:

- **How you respond mentally and emotionally** to the restrictions

- **What support systems you build** around your limitations

- **How you communicate your needs** to medical professionals and loved ones

- **What you focus on within the space you have** (I couldn't hold my baby as much as I wanted, but I could be present when I did hold her)

- **How you plan knowing your body's limits**

It's not about controlling everything. It's about making intentional choices within the space your restrictions allow.

Moving Forward with Physical Restrictions

Physical space (or lack of it) teaches us lessons about acceptance and adaptation. My body set boundaries I couldn't negotiate away, but within those boundaries, I still had movement. I still had choices. I still had the capacity to grow, just not in the ways I'd originally imagined.

Your body may be setting boundaries right now through illness, injury, chronic conditions, or life stages. The question isn't how to eliminate those boundaries but how to create meaningful movement through them.

Energy Management (Not Time Management)

You've probably read a dozen time management books. Downloaded the apps. (I've even tried some apps that college students use to juggle their time.) Color-coded your calendar. And still felt like you're failing.

Here's the truth: time isn't the issue—we all have 24 hours each day. The issue is energy. And a woman's energy doesn't operate on a linear, consistent schedule.

Time management assumes you have the same capacity every day. However, your body knows better. Your energy shifts with your cycle, your stress levels, your caregiving demands, and your emotional load, which starts before you even begin your "real" work.

The problem isn't that you're bad at managing time. The problem is that you're managing the wrong thing. Energy is the real resource—and honoring its rhythms isn't weakness but wisdom.

Here I am, over 40, and I've hit the maturity mark: perimenopause. Energy ebbs and flows had me stuck. I felt like the world around me was moving at top speed, and I couldn't keep up.

The Energy Reality

Physical Energy

Physical energy is determined by sleep, health, hormones, nutrition, and exercise.

My physical capacity naturally varies depending on where I am in my menstrual cycle, whether I'm under deadlines at work, and if I'm trying to juggle home life with everything else.

Emotional Energy

Emotional energy is determined by stress, relationships, mental health, and life circumstances.

Personally, my emotional capacity is contingent on my relationship with my family, my children, and stress at work.

Mental Energy

Mental energy is determined by cognitive load, decision fatigue, and focus demands.

My mental capacity depends on the projects I'm working on and the decisions I have to make that could be life-altering.

The Energy Audit

Let's help you manage your energy. Circle the ones that pertain to you:

Morning Energy: I typically wake up feeling:

- Rested and ready
- Tired but functional
- Exhausted and depleted
- Other: _____

Midday Energy: By afternoon, I'm typically:

- Still going strong
- Starting to fade
- Running on fumes
- Other: _____

Evening Energy: By nighttime, I typically:

- Have energy for family/activities
- Can barely function
- Am completely depleted
- Other: _____

Energy Drains: What depletes my energy fastest?

1.

2.

3.

Energy Restorers: What replenishes my energy?

1.

2.

3.

The Strategy:

Design your life around your energy reality, not an ideal schedule:

High-Energy Tasks:

_____

Do these when:

_____

Medium-Energy Tasks:

_____

Do these when:

_____

Low-Energy Tasks:

_____

Do these when:

_____

Physical Space Reflection Worksheet

Physical Restrictions to Identify

- Health conditions or chronic issues
- Energy limitations
- Sleep quality and quantity
- Physical pain or discomfort
- Body-based trauma or stress
- Pregnancy/fertility considerations
- Age-related changes
- Disability or mobility limitations

Red Flags: Check any that apply:

- ☐ You're constantly exhausted.
- ☐ You're ignoring pain or symptoms.
- ☐ You can't remember the last time you felt good.
- ☐ Your body is giving you clear warning signs.
- ☐ You're sacrificing physical health for other goals.

☐ You feel disconnected from your body.

☐ Physical issues are affecting multiple life areas.

Understanding Your Physical Boundaries

1. From the checklist above: What physical restrictions or limitations are you currently experiencing?

2. Are these restrictions temporary or ongoing? How does knowing this affect your approach?

3.How do these restrictions affect your other life pillars?

➢ Mental:

➢ Emotional:

➢ Spiritual:

➢ Professional:

➢ Relational:

➢ Financial:

➢ Purpose:

Rest and Restore

How do you rest and restore? What do you do daily? Weekly? Monthly? Quarterly? (For example, sleep for eight hours a night, exercise, meditate.) If you're not doing your part to rest and restore your physical body, why not, and what can you start doing? Small steps make a big difference and have a cascading effect on all areas of your life.

Action Steps

1. Based on your reflections, what's one change you can make this week to work with your body rather than against it?

2. Who do you need to communicate with about your physical boundaries (medical professionals, family, employer)?

3. What resources or support systems could help you manage your physical restrictions more effectively?

CHAPTER 4

The Mental Pillar

MENTAL PILLAR: Creating room for new thoughts

When I moved across the country from NY to Carlsbad, California in 2018, my mental space was definitely tested. Growing up in NYC had given me the great fortune of being surrounded by cultures of every kind. Late-night bodegas were open if I wanted to grab a snack. Nightclubs stayed open until the sun was minutes from rising. The subway could take me from one borough to another at any hour. The hustle and bustle of the city streets felt like the heartbeat of life itself.

Most of all, I was surrounded by family and friends. Going to see my sisters and my mom was just a short 20-minute walk at one point. Weekend gatherings at a cousin's house with food and music were something we were used to. That proximity wasn't just convenient. It was part of my identity. I was a New Yorker. I knew how to handle the chaos, how to read the energy, how to find people in a city of millions. It was the good, the bad, and the ugly all in one place!

When I moved to Carlsbad, I felt like my world went to sleep and I woke up in a dream.

Everything was so picturesque. Each view was like a postcard I'd bought on vacation: the ocean, the mountains, the palm trees, the perfect weather. I couldn't believe this was real life and not a dream. Mentally, though, I was restricted by the shift.

There were no spontaneous visits with my sisters. The vibrant cultural diversity I'd grown up with was replaced by a different kind of community. It was beautiful but unfamiliar. The energy was calm where I was used to chaos. The pace was slow where I'd thrived on speed. I had to mentally change my thoughts about what "normal" meant. Without my family and friends close by, and without the culture and community I'd always known, things were very different. My mind kept telling me that different was not completely great!

As a woman making a major life decision, I faced a mental restriction many women know: the guilt of prioritizing career advancement over family needs and vice versa. Then there was the guilt of missing my New York family. Growing up, I was always under the impression that women should seamlessly manage everyone's happiness, never admitting when our own mental adjustment needed to take some time. The mental shift wasn't just about accepting California. It was about giving myself permission to struggle publicly, to not have it all figured out immediately, to admit I was learning a new way to be. That mental flexibility challenged the "women should make it look easy" narrative I'd internalized.

"She remembered who she was and the game changed." Lalah Delia

What Mental Restrictions Teach Us

The hardest part of the move wasn't the physical distance. It was the mental prison I created by clinging to old definitions of home, belonging, and possibility. I was standing in paradise, but my thoughts were keeping me trapped. I immersed myself in work, putting in long hours and consecutive days without taking time off. I used it as my personal excuse to create my norm. Hospitality was familiar to me, so I figured that if I could create a sense of belonging at work, I would be able to change my mind about my new surroundings.

This is what mental space restrictions look like: when your thoughts, not your circumstances, become the barrier.

1) **How to recognize when your thoughts are creating unnecessary restrictions**

For months after the move, I thought the problem was Carlsbad. It was too quiet, too calm, too different. But the real problem was my mental framework. I believed that life could only feel full in the context I'd always known.

Signs your thoughts are creating unnecessary restrictions:

- You find yourself saying, "I can't" when the reality is, "I don't know yet."

- You compare your new situation to the past rather than seeing it on its own terms.

- You focus on what's missing instead of what's present.

- You tell yourself a story about what's "normal" or "right" that limits your current possibilities.

- You resist adapting because it feels like losing part of yourself.

I kept thinking that real community looked like walking to my sister's house. However, that thought was a restriction, not a reality. Community could look different in Carlsbad; I just had to open my mind to see it.

How to recognize it:

Ask yourself: Is this circumstance impossible, or does my current thinking make it impossible? Often, the constraint isn't the situation; it's the story we are telling ourselves about what the situation means.

1) **Strategies for adapting your mindset when your environment changes dramatically**

My mental breakthrough came when I stopped trying to recreate New York in California and started asking, "What does this place offer that I couldn't access before?"

Reframe the change:

- Instead of thinking, "I've lost the city's energy," I learned to think, "I've gained space to hear myself think."

- Instead of "My family is too far away," I reframed it as "I'm building independence while maintaining connection."

- Instead of "This isn't diverse enough," I explored "What new perspectives can I learn here?"

Create new mental categories:

My mind wanted to sort everything as better or worse than New York. I had to create a new category: different, and valuable in its own way.

Build bridges, not walls:

Rather than completely abandoning my New York identity, I learned to integrate my NY swag into my Cali life! I was still a New Yorker at heart. I just learned to be a New Yorker who also appreciated a good sunset beach walk.

Find the familiar in the new:

I couldn't walk to see my sisters, but I could video call them while watching the Cali sunset. I couldn't ride the subway to a different borough, but I could ride the train to downtown San Diego and take it up north to Anaheim to go to Disneyland.

1) Ways to create mental flexibility when physical change feels overwhelming

The physical change happened overnight: we packed, we moved, we unpacked. But mental adaptation takes time. I had to give myself permission to be mentally flexible rather than demanding instant adjustment.

Practice mental flexibility:

- **Release the "should":** I kept thinking, "I should love this immediately" or "I should be over New York by now."

Those "shoulds" created mental rigidity. When I released them, I could actually experience where I was.

- **Allow both/and thinking:** I could miss New York AND appreciate Carlsbad. I could feel lonely AND be building new connections. Mental flexibility means holding multiple truths at once.

- **Create small experiments:** Instead of deciding, "I'll never fit in here," I tested small hypotheses: "What happens if I join the locals? What if I explore one new neighborhood?" Each small experiment expanded my mental map of possibility.

- **Journal the transition:** Writing helped me externalize my thoughts and see patterns. I noticed when I was making things horrific in my mind but, in reality, it was just about changing my mindset.

- **Seek diverse perspectives:** Talking to others who'd made similar moves helped me see that my mental struggle was normal, not a sign that I'd made the wrong choice.

The Shift that Changed Everything

One day, a few months into living in Carlsbad, I was walking to the beach—something I never did in New York from my home. I realized I wasn't trying to find New York in California anymore. I was simply present in California, appreciating it for what it was. My thoughts had shifted from "This isn't home" to "This is a different kind of home."

That mental shift didn't erase my love for New York. It didn't mean I stopped missing my family. It meant I stopped living in a mental prison of comparison and started living in the reality of where I was, appreciating my new kind of home.

As the saying goes: "Change your thoughts, change your life."

Moving Forward with Mental Restrictions

Mental restrictions are perhaps the most powerful because they're invisible. No one can see them but you. They're also the most within your control. You cannot always change your circumstances, but you can always work on changing how you think about your circumstances.

When your environment changes, whether through a move, a job change, a relationship shift, or any major life transition, your thoughts will initially resist. That's normal. The question is: will you stay trapped in those resistant thoughts, or will you create the mental flexibility to adapt?

Mental Space Reflection Worksheet: Understanding Your Mental Restrictions

Mental Restrictions to Identify

- "I can't" thoughts: the stories you tell yourself about what you're not good at

- Thought habits that keep you stuck: worry spirals, worst-case scenarios, comparison traps

- Learning challenges or gaps: what you don't know and how you feel about it (for example, "I should already know this")

- Mental wellness/brain chemistry: anxiety, depression, ADHD, or other conditions that affect how your brain functions

- Thought patterns about yourself as a woman

- Internalized messages from family/culture: thoughts that aren't yours, things you were taught growing up

- Decision-making patterns: how you make choices or avoid them (do you decide quickly or agonize? trust yourself or always ask others?)

- Mental bandwidth and what's taking up space in your brain: all the things you're trying to remember, manage, and track mentally at once

Red Flags: (Check all that apply)

☐ You can't stop negative thought loops.

☐ You assume the worst about your abilities.

☐ You're mentally exhausted from overthinking.

☐ You can't focus or concentrate.

☐ You're making decisions out of fear.

☐ You compare yourself constantly to others.

☐ You can't see possibilities, only problems.

1. From the red flags above, what major change or transition are you currently experiencing or have recently experienced?

2. What thoughts keep running through your mind about this change?

3.Which of these thoughts feel helpful, and which feel like they're holding you back?

Recognizing Thought-Created Restrictions

1. What do you find yourself saying "I can't" about? For each one, ask: Is this actually impossible, or does my current thinking make it feel impossible?

"I can't..." → Reality check:

2. What are you comparing your current situation to? How is that comparison affecting your ability to see possibilities in your present?

3. What stories are you telling yourself about what's "normal" or "right" that might be limiting your current possibilities?

Adapting Your Mindset

1. Looking at your current situation, what does it offer that you couldn't access before? (Even if it's hard to see right now, push yourself to find at least three things.)

2. How can you reframe your thoughts about this change?

Instead of thinking: _____

I could think: _____

3. What aspects of your former situation/identity can you integrate with your new one rather than seeing them as opposing forces?

Creating Mental Flexibility

1. What "shoulds" are you placing on yourself about how you should feel or adapt? What happens if you release those expectations?

2. What small experiment could you try this week to test a new way of thinking about your situation?

3. Complete this sentence in multiple ways:

"I can feel _____ AND _____." (Practice holding multiple truths at once.)

Action Steps

1. What's one mental habit you want to change this week?

2. Who could you talk to who has managed a similar transition successfully?

3. How will you practice noticing your thoughts without immediately accepting them as truth?

Reflection Question:

If your thoughts weren't restricting you, what would you do differently right now?

CHAPTER 5

The Emotional Pillar

EMOTIONAL PILLAR: Developing the right balance of connection and independence

When we moved to California in 2018, my oldest daughter stayed behind to finish middle school in NY. A few months later, she joined us, and I was thrilled. Here, I could provide a different quality of life for her and give her a new perspective: a different high school experience. One that I'd had to travel far from home to somewhat have.

She could walk to school on to a beautiful campus where the football team and sports were the highlight of the school.

Everything I'd hoped to give her was right there. Imagine my teenage daughter, the only darker-skinned girl in the class. She had curly hair and walked around school in her Jordans. She really brought her NY to Cali. Her style, her confidence, and her authenticity were evident. Then... she got bullied.

My daughter, whom I'd moved across the country to give her a better experience, was facing her own environmental restrictions. She was different in a place that didn't celebrate difference the way New York did. She did her best to move through it, to adapt, to find her place, but the emotional toll was real.

She eventually switched to online school, and all she dreamed about was moving back to New York as quickly as possible. She graduated a year early. I could have insisted she stay. I could have told her she needed to give California more time, that she would adjust eventually, that our family needed to be together. Instead, I let her fulfill her dream of going to esthetician school during her gap year, work as an esthetician, and then start college in New York.

It was the hardest emotional lesson I've ever learned. I had to let her go.

As a mother, the emotional restriction of letting my daughter go carried the weight of every societal message about what "good mothers" do. Was I being a "bad mother"? Good mothers sacrifice their own needs. Good mothers don't choose "career over family"—and if they do, they certainly don't let their children leave again. The emotional work of separating my feelings from her needs, of supporting her independence despite my sadness, challenged the narrative that women, especially mothers, should derive our identity and worth from proximity to those we love.

What Emotional Restrictions Teach Us

I thought providing physical proximity (having my daughter with me in California) was the same as providing connection. But the emotional space doesn't work that way. Sometimes, the most loving thing you can do is create distance. Sometimes, holding on too tightly is what actually breaks the bond.

1) How to maintain emotional connection while honoring independence

When my daughter first told me she wanted to move back to New York, every fiber of my soul wanted to say, "No." I'd just gotten her here. How could she want to leave?

Her independence wasn't a rejection of me or our connection. It was her becoming who she needed to be.

Here's the shift I had to make:

From: "If she leaves, we'll lose our connection."

To: "If I support her independence, our connection can deepen."

The 3,000-mile space between us became a teacher about connection that doesn't require proximity. We eventually became closer than we were when she lived under my roof.

The Emotional pillar is about developing the right balance between connection and independence, and understanding that healthy relationships need both.

The Strategy that Changed Everything

I had to separate my feelings from my daughter's decisions. Yes, I felt sad about her leaving. Yes, I worried about her leaving. Yes, I worried about her being so far away. Yes, I missed her physical presence. Those were my feelings to manage, not her burden to fix by staying.

Practical strategies for working through your emotions:

- Name your emotions without making them the other person's responsibility: "I'm going to miss you so much. Let's figure out how we'll stay close" vs. "How could you leave me?!" What exact emotion are you feeling? Sad, angry, disappointed, etc.

- Understand your emotions without judgment; give yourself grace. Yes, I was sad she was leaving, but I helped her plan the move and celebrated milestones like getting accepted into the school, even though every part of it hurt. You're just a human going through emotions, and that's okay.

- Work through your emotions, whether through journaling, positive self-talk, friend therapy, or professional therapy. Not working through negative emotions can block your overall growth and prevent you reaching your goals, so you want to find ways to work through them.

"There is no greater agony than bearing an untold story inside you." Maya Angelou

Emotional Space Reflection Worksheet: Understanding Your Emotional Restrictions

Emotional Restrictions to Identify

- Suppressed or unexpressed emotions: emotions you push down, hide, or pretend don't exist

- Emotional regulation challenges: when your emotions feel too big or out of control, such as crying too much

- Trauma responses: automatic reactions from previous hurt that affect how you respond now

- Emotional labor (especially unpaid): the energy you spend reading the room, keeping the peace, anticipating needs, and making others comfortable

- Caregiver burnout: exhaustion from taking care of everyone but yourself

- Grief or loss processing: unprocessed sadness that's still weighing on you

- Emotional availability: how much emotional capacity you have for managing everything else

- Vulnerability capacity: how much of your authentic self you can safely reveal to others without feeling unsafe or overwhelmed.

Red Flags: (check all that apply)

☐ You're numb or disconnected.

☐ You cry more than usual (or can't cry at all).

☐ You're emotionally exhausted.

☐ You can't handle others' emotions.

☐ You feel empty or hollow.

☐ You're using food/alcohol/work to avoid feelings.

☐ You snap or rage unexpectedly.

1. In what relationship(s) do you feel emotional restriction or tension right now?

2. What are you afraid will happen if you create more emotional space in this relationship?

Connection vs. Control Assessment

1.Think about a relationship where you feel tension. Complete these statements honestly:

I'm holding on because: _____

If I let go, I fear: _____

What I really want for this person: _____

Are you confusing proximity/control with connection? How can you tell?

Honoring Independence

1. In what ways might you be trying to control someone else's choices "for their own good"?

2. What would it look like to support this person's independence while maintaining connection?

3. What makes it difficult for you to trust someone else's choices about their own life?

Loving Without Controlling

1. Complete this reframe:

Instead of: "If you loved me, you would…"

I can think: _____

2. What emotions are you experiencing that you might be making someone else's responsibility to fix?

3. How can you manage these emotions yourself?

4. Where do you need to separate your feelings from someone else's decisions?

Creating Healthy Boundaries

1. What boundary would strengthen a current relationship, even though it feels scary to establish it?

2. What would change if you believed that distance (physical or emotional) doesn't have to diminish love?

3. In what relationship could you shift from obligatory interaction to chosen connection?

Building Confidence in Your Bonds

1. What evidence do you have that your important relationships can survive independence and space?

2. How has trying to control someone actually weakened your connection with them?

3. What would become possible in your relationships if you led with trust instead of fear?

Action Steps

1. What's one way you can honor someone's independence this week while maintaining connection?

2. What emotional boundary do you need to establish to strengthen (not weaken) a relationship?

3. Complete this commitment:

This week, I will practice loving without controlling by:

_____

Reflection Question:

If you fully trusted that your relationships could survive independence and distance, what would you do differently?

CHAPTER 6:

The Spiritual Pillar

SPIRITUAL PILLAR: Finding purpose through limitations

A Note on Spiritual Paths

This chapter reflects my journey of moving through restrictions by building a personal practice to find purpose through them. Your spiritual journey may look different. You might be deeply connected to a faith tradition, find community in church, or follow a completely different spiritual path.

The framework here is about recognizing when you're operating without a clear map and learning to trust yourself anyway. Whether that applies to you or not, the principle remains:

spiritual movement happens when you stop waiting for permission and start trusting what resonates as true for you.

For some, that means deepening commitment to their faith tradition. For others, like me, it means building something unconventional. Both are valid.

"Sometimes the bad things that happen in our lives put us directly on the path to the best things that will ever happen to us." Nicole Reed

Finding Your Own Way to Meaning

Spirituality doesn't require a religious institution. For me, it's about recognizing that life's hardest moments—the ones I can't control, can't fix, can't escape—often reveal a deeper purpose than anything I could have planned. My spiritual restriction has been this: I've had to learn to find meaning within limitations instead of waiting for them to disappear.

In 2009, a few years after my wedding and a short time after I purchased my first home, my dad succumbed to his physical restrictions caused by alcoholism and drug abuse many years earlier. He'd been in the hospital for two weeks. I took time off from work to make sure I could visit and spend time with him each day, rotating with my family members so he was never alone.

That particular morning, before I visited, I prayed. I prayed that my dad wouldn't suffer anymore. I had faith that whatever was meant for him would be for him. That there was a plan beyond what I could see or control.

I had to drop my daughter at daycare before catching the bus to the hospital. The first bus came later than its regular time. Then I missed the second bus, so I had to wait for the next one. As I walked to the hospital, frustrated because I was late, I had a sense of something not being right. When I got upstairs to my father's room, I peeked in to make sure it was a good time for me to visit, but all I could see were his legs and feet on the bed. The head nurse, who was always so rude and mean to everyone, was suddenly very sweet, running up to me before I fully walked into my dad's room. "I was just trying to call you," she said. "Your father died a few minutes ago." I had just seen him the night before. He was speaking with us. Laughing. Present.

I cried hysterically. If only I'd been a few minutes earlier. If only I hadn't missed that bus. Then I could have said goodbye to my dad. The guilt overwhelmed me in those first few minutes. The head nurse asked me to step inside a conference room to make phone calls to the rest of the family. I was the one who had to call my mom, my sisters, my dad's siblings, and the list went on. I sat in that empty room, making call after devastating call, feeling life had no meaning.

The Realization

For weeks after my father's death, I was haunted by those missed buses. Why couldn't I have been there? Why didn't I get to say goodbye? Then, slowly, a realization came. I'd prayed that very morning for my father not to suffer. He didn't die with his daughter watching, helpless to save him. Whether he could control that timing or not, I came to believe there was a purpose in it.

Limitations force you to confront what you truly believe about meaning.

When we face limitations we absolutely cannot change—loss, career pivots, uncertainties completely beyond our control—

we're forced to ask: Is there meaning beyond what we can see and touch and manage? When we can't control outcomes, we either find spiritual meaning or collapse into meaninglessness.

Connecting to Other Pillars

Physical Pillar Connection: During my pregnancy bed rest and blood pressure emergency, I couldn't control my body. I had to surrender to what my body was telling me, which deepened my faith that something larger was at work. The physical limitation of potentially dying during childbirth forced the same spiritual question: Is there purpose I can't see?

Relational Pillar Connection: When my oldest daughter told me she wanted to move back to New York, I had to trust she was meant for that path, even when it hurt. I couldn't control her choices or force her to stay. The limitation of loving someone while letting them go required spiritual trust that her journey served a purpose beyond my understanding.

Professional Pillar Connection: Being "the first" female Latina Director in a few of my career roles wasn't just career advancement; it carried spiritual weight. I felt called to that role, positioned for a reason. That belief shaped my decision-making differently than ambition alone would have.

Purpose lives in how I move through these moments, not in avoiding them.

Strategies for Discovering Purpose Within Limitations

Stop waiting for the limitation to end before seeking meaning.

For months after my father's death, I tried to find purpose around the loss. I threw myself into work. I focused on my family. I stayed busy. The grief and guilt followed me everywhere. The breakthrough came when I stopped trying to go *around* the loss and started looking for purpose *within* it.

The meaning wasn't waiting beyond the grief. The purpose was being revealed through the grief, within the loss, because of the restriction.

Ask what the limitation is revealing.

My father's death revealed:

- **Time is precious:** How fragile life is
- **Love matters now:** The importance of expressing love while we can
- **Priorities become clear:** What truly matters when everything else is stripped away

Look for transformation, not resolution.

I'm not over losing my father. But I've been transformed by it in ways that give my life deeper purpose.

Create space for the questions (not rushing past "why")

In that conference room, stripped of control, I sat with the question: "Is there something greater than all of this?" I didn't rush past it. I didn't force an answer. I sat in the space between knowing and not knowing.

Look for patterns (timing, synchronicities, things aligning unexpectedly).

The timing of missing those buses. The nurse who was always rude suddenly being kind. My daughter being born the following year, carrying so much of my father's warmth and presence. These weren't coincidences. They were breadcrumbs pointing toward something larger.

Connection to professional journey: Missing that first Director position at the Carlsbad resort, then being offered it when the new director didn't work out. The timing felt orchestrated, as if I was being positioned for opportunities when I was ready for them.

These aren't tricks to make yourself feel better. They're ways to read what's happening and find your role in it.

Practicing Spirituality Through What You Can Control

After my father's death, how I showed up changed.

I couldn't control his death. I couldn't control the timing. I couldn't get my goodbye. But I could control how I moved through the loss and what I did with what it revealed:

- I became more intentional with my family.

- I stopped postponing conversations that mattered.

- I recognized moments of grace: small things that felt placed exactly when I needed them.

- I began to see life not as something to control but as something to participate in with gratitude.

This is how I practice spirituality now:

- **Through presence:** Showing up fully in the moment I'm in

- **Through trust:** Believing I'm positioned in scenarios for a reason

- **Through recognizing:** Seeing that my job is to show up well within those scenarios

Connection to pregnancy restrictions: I couldn't control my blood pressure or the preeclampsia. But I could show up for my body's needs. I could trust the medical guidance. I could recognize that this limitation was teaching me to surrender.

Your job is to show up well within the limitations you can't change.

Spirituality isn't about having all the answers or never questioning why hard things happen. It's about finding purpose not by avoiding limitations but by moving through them with faith that there's meaning woven into even the hardest moments.

When circumstances strip everything else away—control, plans, certainty—what remains is the question: How will I show up?

Spiritual Space Reflection Worksheet: Your Spiritual Journey

Spiritual Restrictions to Identify

- Values misalignment: living against what you believe in

- Purpose confusion or crisis: not knowing your "why"

- Meaning-making challenges: struggling to find purpose in your plan

- Big questions about life, death and what matters

- Spiritual practices (or lack thereof): missing the rituals that ground you

- Connection to something larger: a sense of being alone, unsupported by anything beyond yourself

- Legacy considerations: what you'll leave behind

- Contribution vs. consumption balance: taking vs. giving

Red Flags: (check all that apply)

- ☐ Life feels meaningless.

- ☐ You've lost connection to what matters.

- ☐ You're going through the motions.

- ☐ You feel spiritually empty.

- ☐ Your values and actions don't align.

☐ You have no sense of purpose.

☐ Everything feels hollow.

Reflecting on Your Spiritual Limitations

1. Looking at the red flags that you checked, which of them feel completely beyond your control?

2. Do you feel that there's a way to move through these restrictions if you try?

3. Have you had a situation in your past where you were able to move past a restriction and it gave you a spiritual understanding? Complete this reflection:

- At the time, this limitation felt:

  _____

- Looking back, I can see that it taught me:

  _____

The Space Between Crisis and Understanding

1. Looking back at a difficult restriction in your life, what spiritual truth did it reveal that you might not have discovered otherwise?

2. When you couldn't control the outcome, what question did you find yourself asking? (For example, "Is there something greater at work?" "Why me?" "What's the point?")

3. How long did it take for any realization or meaning to emerge? (Days? Weeks? Months? Years? Still waiting?)

Recognizing Patterns and Timing

1. Have there been moments when timing, circumstances, or events aligned in ways you couldn't have planned? What did that reveal?

2. What coincidences or synchronicities have you noticed in your hardest moments that you initially dismissed?

3. Complete this prompt: When I can't rely on my own power or understanding, I find: _____

The Principle in Your Life

1. When you face limitations, you absolutely cannot change, what do you turn to for meaning?

2. Have you ever experienced a moment where finding spiritual meaning felt like the only alternative to collapsing into meaning-lessness? Describe it.

Strategies for Discovering Purpose Within Limitations

Stop Waiting for the Limitation to End

1. What current limitation are you trying to get past before you can find purpose again?

2. Where have you been looking for meaning *around* a limitation rather than *within* it?

3. What if you stopped trying to move past it? What purpose might be revealed within this limitation right now?

Ask What the Limitation Is Revealing

For each of your major life limitations, ask: "What is this revealing about..."

1. Time: What has this taught you about how precious time is?

2. Fragility: What has this shown you about how fragile life/health/relationships/security can be?

3. Love: What has this revealed about what matters most to you?

4. Priorities: What has this clarified about how you want to spend your energy?

Look for Transformation, Not Resolution

1. What loss or limitation are you NOT over but have been transformed by?

2. How might this restriction be transforming you in ways that serve a larger purpose?

3. List three ways in which you've changed because of a limitation you faced (not despite it):

I became more _____.

I stopped _____.

I started _____.

Notice What Restrictions Make Possible

1. What has a limitation made possible in your life that wouldn't have happened otherwise?

2. Complete these prompts:

Because I couldn't _____, I became more

_____.

This restriction forced me to _____, which led to

_____.

Look for Patterns Across Your Life

1. Looking at the major limitations in your life, what patterns do you notice? What might they be pointing you toward?

2. Where do you see threads connecting across different restrictions you've faced?

3. Complete this commitment: This week, I will show up well within my limitations by:

Being present when _____

Trusting that _____

Recognizing _____

Integration Across Pillars

1. How does your spiritual belief (or lack of clear structure) affect your major life decisions?

2. Where has a limitation in another pillar (Physical, Emotional, Relational, Professional) deepened your spiritual understanding?

3. Which pillar are you currently struggling with? How might spiritual trust help you move through it?

Final Reflection

If you fully trusted that your current limitations are part of a larger purpose you can't fully see yet, what would you do differently today?

CHAPTER 7

The Professional Pillar

PROFESSIONAL PILLAR: Aligning work with values

In 2013, After many years of climbing the hospitality ladder, from café attendant to shift supervisor to director positions at hotels, I made a hard decision: I was going to open a home daycare.

To the outside world, it looked like I was stepping back. Stepping down. Giving up everything I'd worked for.

However, what seemed like stepping back was stepping into a different kind of leadership. It was one that would teach me more about balancing stability and flexibility than any role ever had.

"I had to make my own living and my own opportunity. But I made it! Don't sit down and wait for the opportunities to come. Get up and make them." Madam C. J. Walker

Why I Made the Change

The decision came down to one painful realization: I felt like I'd chosen my career over being with my oldest daughter. While I was managing properties and building my resume, my family was spending time with her. They knew her daily rhythms, her favorite stories, her little quirks. I was missing out.

I didn't want to repeat that pattern with my younger daughter.

I also couldn't just stop working. We needed the income. I needed the professional fulfillment. I needed to use my skills and experience in meaningful ways.

As a woman in hospitality leadership, I'd fought hard to climb the ladder in male-dominated operations roles. Choosing to step away for a home daycare felt like confirming every stereotype about women and career commitment: "She couldn't handle it." "She chose family over ambition." "That's why we shouldn't promote women to leadership." The professional restriction wasn't just about giving myself permission to redefine success despite knowing others would see it as "giving up." Opening the daycare was leading unrestricted because I refused to let others' gendered narratives about ambition and motherhood dictate what professional success could look like for me.

The professional restriction I faced was this: How do you create career stability and financial security while also having the flexibility to be present with your children?

Traditional career advice says you can't have both. You either climb the ladder or you step off. You either commit to your career or you commit to your family. It's hard to have work–life balance. It definitely takes a village. I was lucky enough to have my sister take the lead in the daycare before I transitioned full-time.

I decided to work through that restriction instead of accepting it as final.

What Professional Space Teaches Us

Opening the home daycare wasn't about abandoning my professional identity. It was about translating everything I'd learned in hospitality into a different context, one that balanced stability (consistent income, using my skills) with flexibility (being home with my daughters, setting my own schedule).

How to Redefine Professional Success on Your Own Terms

For years, professional success meant one thing in my mind: climbing higher. More responsibility. Bigger properties. Better titles. That's what everyone around me was measuring success by.

But success on someone else's terms often means restriction on your own.

The shift I had to make:

From: "Success means advancing in a traditional career path"

To: "Success means creating work that aligns with my current life priorities"

What redefining success looked like practically:

I used my genuine hospitality skills to bring parents in. Within the first month of opening, we'd maxed out the ratio of kids to caregiver we could legally have. My years of customer service, operations management, and team leadership translated perfectly. I was just in a completely different setting.

I ran the daycare side by side with my sister. We created systems, managed schedules, handled finances, marketed our services, and maintained compliance with regulations. It was entrepreneurship that required every professional skill I'd developed, just applied differently. I also had the privilege of having my cousin work in the daycare part time.

The revelation:

I can honestly say that those were the best career days of my life. Not because of the money. I made far less than I had in hospitality leadership. It was because of the experience. The children. My children. The creative freedom. The autonomy. The alignment between my work and my values. The integrity of knowing that we were caring for these children as if they were our own.

How to redefine professional success on your own terms:

- Separate achievement from advancement: Success doesn't have to mean climbing. Sometimes, it means creating something that fits your life better.

- Define your own metrics: Instead of titles and salaries, I measured success by:

  - Time with my daughters

- Flexibility in my schedule
- Creative control
- Impact on children's lives
- Quality of life

- Give yourself permission to pivot: Your past career path doesn't have to dictate your future one. Every skill is transferable if you're creative about application.

- Reject the "all or nothing" narrative: I didn't have to choose between professional fulfillment and family presence. I created a third option that honored both.

Questions to ask yourself:

What does professional success actually mean to me, not to my industry, my family's expectations, or society's standards?

If I could design work that perfectly fits my current life season, what would it look like?

Strategies for Creating Career Flexibility Without Sacrificing Financial Stability

The biggest fear I faced when considering the daycare was financial. Could I really make this work? Could we afford to have me leave a stable salary?

I took a strategic approach:

- Leverage existing skills in new contexts: I didn't start from scratch. I applied years of hospitality, customer service, operations, and leadership skills to the daycare. This gave me a competitive advantage and faster success.

- Start with a tested model: Home daycare had proven demand and clear regulations. I wasn't inventing something completely new; rather, I was entering an established field with my unique strengths.

- Create multiple income streams within one business: The daycare provided steady weekly income from regular clients, plus the flexibility to take on occasional drop-ins after school for additional revenue.

- Maintain professional development: Even though I'd left traditional hospitality, I stayed current with early childhood education and business management. I also continued building skills that served my current work and kept me marketable if I ever wanted to return to corporate roles.

The reality check:

Did I make as much money as I did managing in hotels? No. But when I factored in the following, the financial equation looked completely different:

- No commute costs

- No work wardrobe expenses

- No childcare costs (I was providing it)

- Weekends and holidays off for the first time in years

- Time with my family that I'd always wished for

Stability isn't just about salary size; it's about sustainable income that supports your actual life needs and priorities.

Strategies for creating flexibility with stability:

- Calculate the true costs and benefits: Look beyond salary to total life costs and quality of life gains.

- Create predictable income with flexible delivery: The daycare had set hours and regular clients (stability), but I controlled the schedule and could close for family needs if necessary (flexibility).

- Build expertise that transfers: Everything I learned running the daycare—small business operations, marketing, financial management, team coordination—enhanced my professional toolkit.

- Design escape routes: I maintained my hospitality network and skills so I could return if circumstances changed, which they eventually did. Flexibility includes the ability to pivot again if needed.

Ways to Translate Your Skills Across Completely Different Professional Contexts

The assumption people make is that hospitality skills only work in hospitality, and that business skills only work in business. But that's the restriction talking.

Skills are transferable when you understand their core function:

- What I thought I was good at: Managing hotel operations, coordinating teams, ensuring guest satisfaction in properties

- What I was actually good at: Creating welcoming environments, managing complex logistics, building trust with clients, leading teams through challenges, maintaining high standards under pressure

Those core skills worked just as well—maybe better—in a home daycare setting.

How I translated specific skills:

- Guest relations → Parent relations: The same principles of listening, anticipating needs, clear communication, and building trust applied perfectly.

- Operations management → Daycare systems: Scheduling, inventory management, safety protocols, quality control—all directly transferable.

- Team leadership → Running a business with other team members: Delegation, conflict resolution, shared vision, complementary strengths—same leadership skills, different team.

- Crisis management → Handling childhood emergencies: Staying calm under pressure, making quick decisions, communicating with stakeholders—exact same skill set.

- Marketing/sales → Filling enrollment: Understanding target audience, communicating value proposition, building reputation through referrals—identical approach.

The mindset shift required:

From: "I'm a hospitality professional, that's what I do."

To: "I'm skilled at creating excellent experiences and managing complex operations. I can apply that anywhere."

How to translate your skills to new contexts:

- Identify the core function, not just the job title: What are you actually doing beneath the industry-specific language?

- Look for parallel challenges: Every field has customer service, operations, leadership, and problem-solving. The details differ, but the skills transfer.

- Practice describing your skills in universal terms: Instead of "I managed a 100-room hotel," say, "I coordinated operations for a high-volume service business requiring precision, customer satisfaction, and team coordination."

- Give yourself permission to be a beginner in specifics while being an expert in fundamentals: I didn't know everything about early childhood education, but I knew everything about running excellent operations and serving clients. I could learn the specifics.

I went through this same exercise when I decided to do life coaching full-time.

The Professional Pillar in Practice

The Professional pillar is about building a career that balances stability and flexibility. Not one or the other: both.

For me, that meant:

- Stability: Consistent income, using proven skills, sustainable business model

- Flexibility: Being home with my daughters, controlling my schedule, creative autonomy, weekends and holidays off

Opening the daycare didn't mean abandoning my professional self. It meant finding a professional expression that fit my whole life, not just my resume.

Years later, when my youngest daughter was school age, I returned to hospitality in leadership roles. The daycare years didn't set me back; they enhanced me. I had entrepreneurial experience, small business management, and proof that I could succeed in completely different contexts.

The lesson: Professional restrictions often aren't about lack of options. They're about lack of permission to design work differently. When you give yourself that permission and get creative about translating your skills, you discover that stability and flexibility aren't opposing forces. They're both possible when you stop accepting someone else's definition of what a career should look like.

"I've learned that making a 'living' is not the same thing as making a 'life.'" Maya Angelou

Professional Space Reflection Worksheet: Understanding Your Professional Situation

Professional Restrictions to Identify

- Career advancement barriers: obstacles preventing promotion, growth, or moving up
- Gender-based limitations: being held back because you're a woman (bias and assumptions)
- Skill or credential gaps: missing qualifications or experience
- Industry-specific challenges: unique barriers in your field
- Work–life integration issues: can't make work fit with the rest of your life
- Income limitations: not making enough money

- Professional identity crisis: Wondering, "Who am I without this job/title?"

- Workplace discrimination or microaggressions: daily slights like being talked over, "jokes" about your identity, assumptions about your competence

Red Flags: (check all that apply)

☐ You dread going to work.

☐ You're being overlooked for advancement.

☐ You're dealing with discrimination.

☐ Your work doesn't align with your values.

☐ You've outgrown your role.

☐ You're sacrificing too much for your career.

☐ Your industry is changing and you're not.

Self-Reflection on the Above Check-Marked Red Flags

1. What does professional success currently mean to you? (Be honest: not what it "should" mean, but what it actually means right now.)

2. Where does that definition come from? (Your industry, family expectations, societal standards, your own values?)

3. What professional restrictions are you currently facing?

Redefining Success on Your Own Terms

1. If you could design work that perfectly fit your current life season and priorities, what would it look like?

2. What professional metrics actually matter to you beyond title and salary?

Quality of life factors I value:

Impact/fulfillment factors I value:

Practical factors I need:

3. Complete this statement:

I've been measuring success by _____, but what I actually want is _____.

2. What would give you permission to redefine professional success on your own terms?

Creating Flexibility with Stability

1. What skills from your current/past work are actually transferable to different contexts?

Core skills beneath my job title:

2. What fears do you have about creating more flexibility in your career?

3. Calculate your true career costs:

Current income: _____

Minus: Commute costs, work wardrobe, childcare, meals out, etc.: _____

Plus: Life quality factors (time, energy, stress level, family presence): _____

What does this reveal about your actual financial situation?

4. What would a career need to provide to give you both stability AND flexibility?

Translating Your Skills

1. Describe your core professional skills without using industry-specific language:

Instead of: "I do [job-specific task]."

Core skill: "I'm skilled at [universal function]."

2. What completely different professional contexts might need the skills you have?

3. What's one way in which you could apply your professional expertise in a non-traditional setting?

Exploring Options

1. If traditional career advancement isn't the only path, what other options exist?

- Side business using existing skills
- Freelance/consulting
- Different industry, same skills
- Entrepreneurship
- Portfolio career (multiple part-time roles)
- Other: _____

2. What small experiment could you run to test a different professional approach without fully committing?

Action Steps

1. What's one way in which you could create more flexibility in your current work situation this month?

2. What skill translation exercise could you practice this week? (Describe what you do in universal rather than industry-specific terms.)

3. Who do you know who has successfully balanced stability and flexibility in their career? What could you learn from their path?

Reflection Questions

1. If professional success was measured only by quality of life and impact, not title or salary, how would you rate your current career?

2. What would you do professionally if you gave yourself full per mission to design it yourself?

CHAPTER 8

The Relational Pillar

RELATIONAL PILLAR: Building relationships that enable growth

My mother was living in California with me and my family. For a few days, she'd been saying she wasn't feeling too good. She had an earache or an infection, a fever, nothing that seemed too concerning to her.

One day after work, I went into her room to check on her and noticed half of her face was drooping.

"We need to go to the emergency room right away," I told her. After two emergency room visits and consultation with a doctor who was a close family friend, she was diagnosed with shingles and Ramsay Hunt syndrome. The condition stripped her of her balance. She couldn't chew. She couldn't walk. Half of her face was paralyzed. I was distraught. How could this have happened? My strong, resilient mother was suddenly completely dependent.

"There is no limit to what we, as women, can accomplish." Michelle Obama

I became her caregiver. Making smoothies because she couldn't chew solid food. Helping her get dressed. Working with her to regain her balance. My sisters flew out from New York right away to help. We stood with her, taking care of her together.

Mind you, this was still at the tail end of COVID, so there was still lots of mask wearing even in the house; we didn't want to risk getting mom sick with COVID on top of everything else.

Then something unexpected happened. Once mom was able to speak more, she started sharing stories from her past. Not the surface stories we'd heard before, but deep ones. Stories of who she was when she was younger. How her mother migrated here when her and her siblings were young. How her father died of a sudden heart attack when she was just two years old. He was protecting her from kids who'd hurt her by throwing marbles. She spoke about how my dad wooed her, coming over to spend time with her mother every morning. She spoke about his alcoholism and drug use, and how she eventually helped him get clean. She spoke about working in the doll factory with my grandma and taking the bus in Brooklyn late at night to get there. She spoke about her resilience, her relationships, and why she eventually decided to leave my dad, even though he'd been sober for many years by then.

These stories came from a different place because she was sick. Her resilience gave me a different perspective of her, not just as my mother but as a woman, a survivor, a person with her own complex journey.

I wanted to know all these things about her, but she'd never spoken in depth about them before.

As a woman, I'd been taught that maintaining family relationships was part of my responsibility. Caring for my mother revealed something deeper. Women often carry their family's emotional history without fully understanding it. My mother's stories about working in factories, surviving my father's addiction, and making impossible choices about love and survival are women's stories that get lost because we're too busy caregiving to ask the questions. The relational restriction wasn't just about role reversal. It was about claiming space to know my mother as a whole woman with her own complex journey, not just as the person who served our family.

What Relational Space Teaches Us

Just as I learned with my daughter that creating emotional space strengthens bonds, caring for my mother taught me how emergencies can transform relationships across generations. The Emotional and Relational pillars work together. What we feel affects how we relate, and how we relate affects what we feel.

The Relational pillar focuses specifically on how we create relationships that enable growth without losing connection, especially when circumstances force us into new relational patterns.

How Emergencies Can Deepen Rather Than Damage Relationships

My mother's illness could have gone several ways relationally. It could have created resentment (her feeling like a burden, me feeling overwhelmed). It could have reinforced old patterns (reverting to parent–child dynamics, where she directed and I obeyed). It could have created distance (both of us uncomfortable with the role reversal). Instead, it deepened our relationship in ways that wouldn't have been possible without the urgent situation.

Why emergencies can deepen relationships:

- Vulnerability creates authenticity: When my mother couldn't maintain her usual independence and strength, she became more open. The stories she shared weren't ones she would have told when she was in her "normal" role as mother and grandmother. Her vulnerability gave her permission to be fully human with us.

- Shared purpose unites: My sisters and I came together with one focus: to help heal mom. The crisis created a unity of purpose that strengthened not just our relationship with mom but our relationships with each other.

- Role reversal reveals new dimensions: For the first time, I was caring for my mother the way she had cared for me. This shift allowed me to see her differently: not as an all-capable mother, but as a person who needed support, who had her own fears and vulnerabilities, and who had survived so much before I was even born.

Strategies for Creating Understanding Across Generational Divides

Before she got sick, I knew her as "mom": the role she played in my life. Her illness created space for me to know her as a person with her own story, her own struggles, and her own journey that existed long before I was born.

I saw her as the strong mother who'd raised us, made decisions, taken care of us. She was also a woman who'd lost her father at two, who'd helped her partner through addiction, who'd worked in factories and the school board system, who'd made impossible choices about love and survival.

Roles become identities. We get stuck seeing our parents as "parents" rather than as full people with complex histories. This can also mean that we see people as their role or the role they play in our lives, but not really who they are.

- When it comes to relationships, create extended time together with shared purpose. The shared purpose in the situation of my mother's healing removed the pressure to perform or entertain.

- Listen without judgment. In your relationships, the other person may be telling you something very deep about themselves, but you may be judging them. Some of the stories mom shared challenged my childhood understanding of our family history. I had to listen without defending my previous narratives or making her wrong for her choices.

Ways to Embrace Different Relationships in Every Form

My relationship with my mother transformed during those months. The Relational pillar isn't just about one relationship. It's about understanding that relationships take many forms, and that each form has its own value and purpose.

Relationships aren't fixed. The same relationship can take different forms at different times. Trying to keep it in one box creates restrictions.

Multiple forms can coexist. I could be daughter, caregiver, student, and fellow adult all at once. These roles didn't cancel each other out. They enriched the full relationship.

Each form teaches something different. In the traditional mother–daughter relationship, she taught me about parenting. As patient to caregiver, she taught me about vulnerability and grace in receiving help. As woman to woman, she taught me about resilience and survival.

How to Embrace Different Relational Forms

- Let go of rigid role definitions: In this instance, your parent can also be your friend. Your child can also be your teacher. Your sibling can also be your collaborator. Fixed roles create relational restrictions

- Honor transitions: When the relationship shifts form, acknowledge it. In this situation, this could mean simply saying, "This feels different, doesn't it?" Naming it reduces awkwardness and creates space for the new form.

The Relational Pillar in Practice

The Relational pillar is about creating relationships that enable growth without losing connection. My mother's illness forced growth in how I saw her, how we related, and how deep our conversations went. However, we didn't lose connection. If anything, the connections strengthened because we embraced the growth instead of resisting it.

Key Insights

- Relationships are more resilient when we let them take different forms rather than insisting, they stay the same.

- The deepest relational growth often happens during times of restriction and vulnerability.

Connection to Other Pillars

Notice how this relational transformation is connected to other pillars:

- Emotional: Feelings of grief, fear, and love came up during mom's illness.

- Physical: Her physical restriction created space for relational depth.

- Purpose: Caregiving became a profound expression of purpose and meaning.

The pillars aren't isolated. Restrictions and growth in one area ripple through all of the others. Understanding this interconnection helps us see that working through restriction in any pillar creates movement across our entire lives.

Relational Space Reflection Worksheet: Understanding Your Relational Patterns

Relational Restrictions to Identify

- Partnership dynamics

- Family obligations

- Caregiving demands

- Friendship capacity

- Boundary issues

- Communication patterns

- Conflict avoidance or escalation

- Isolation or overwhelm

Red Flags: *(Check all that apply)*

- ☐ You feel alone even in relationships.

- ☐ You can't set boundaries.

- ☐ You're everyone's caregiver with no care for you.

- ☐ Relationships feel transactional.

- ☐ You avoid conflict at all costs.

☐ You have no one to talk to.

☐ Your relationships drain you.

Self-reflecting on any red flag you checked above:

1. How healthy are your key relationships? (1–10) ____

2. What relationship patterns keep repeating?

3. What boundaries need to be set?

4. What relationships are draining you?

5. What relational needs are unmet?

6. Are you relating to important people in your life primarily through fixed roles (parent, child, employee, spouse) rather than as full people?

Urgent Situations and Relationships

1. Think of a time of difficulty you've experienced with someone close to you. Did it damage or deepen the relationship? What made the difference?

2. Is there a current challenge in a relationship that could become a deepening opportunity if approached differently?

How could you shift your approach:

Generational Understanding

1. What do you know about the important people in your life beyond their role in your life?

For a parent/elder: What was their life like before you? What challenges did they face? What choices did they make?

For a child/younger person: What are their dreams, fears, and challenges separate from your hopes for them?

2. What questions have you never asked someone important to you because you assumed you knew the answers or they wouldn't want to share?

3. What would create the time and space for deeper storytelling in your important relationships?

Creating Understanding

1. Complete these reflections about someone important to you:

I see them as: _____.

But they might also be: _____.

2. What judgment or assumption about someone's choices might shift if you understood their full story?

3. How could you create extended, purposeful time with someone you want to understand more deeply?

Embracing Different Relational Forms

1. In what relationship are you trying to maintain a fixed form that no longer fully fits?

2. What different forms could your important relationships take?

Example: A parent–child relationship could also include adult–adult, student–teacher, caregiver–patient, friends, collaborators, etc.

Pick one relationship and list possible forms:

3. What makes it difficult for you to let relationships change form?

4. What becomes possible when you embrace different relational forms instead of insisting on one?

Role Reversal

1. Are you experiencing (or anticipating) any role reversals in important relationships (caring for parents, adult children becoming independent, power shifts at work)?

How are you navigating this: _____

What resistance are you feeling: _____

2. What would it mean to honor the transition instead of fighting it?

Building Connection Through Growth

1. Where in your relationships do you need to:

Create more vulnerability: _____

Allow more authenticity: _____

Make space for deeper conversations: _____

Let go of fixed expectations: _____

2. What shared purpose or challenge could unite you more deeply with someone important to you?

Action Steps

1. What's one question you could ask someone this week to understand their story more deeply?

2. What relationship needs more extended, intentional time together? How will you create that?

3. What relational form shift do you need to embrace rather than resist?

Reflection Questions:

1. If you could see the important people in your life as full, complex humans with their own stories rather than just their roles in your life, how would it change your relationships?

2. What restriction in a relationship might actually be creating space for a deeper form of connection?

CHAPTER 9

The Financial Pillar

FINANCIAL PILLAR: Developing sustainable resource patterns that support your purpose

While working as a department head in a busy NYC hotel when my youngest daughter was still a baby, I faced a financial reality many women know too well: debt overcame income.

I could have just accepted this financial restriction. Instead, I asked: "How can I create additional income doing something that energizes me rather than exhausts me?"

That question led me to professional clown school in the Bronx.

Yes, you read that right. While managing hotel operations, I decided to learn face painting, balloon twisting, and how to create entertainment naturally at children's parties. I created playlists, developed games and activities, and learned how to make kids and parents have a great time together.

I started doing parties for friends and family. The extra income wasn't huge, but it filled a financial void while filling something else I hadn't anticipated: my creative spirit. I was using skills from hospitality (creating experiences, reading the room, managing chaos) in a completely unexpected way.

What Financial Restrictions Teach Us

The Financial pillar isn't just about making more money. It's about developing sustainable resource patterns that support your purpose without sacrificing your values or your energy.

How to Use Creativity to Overcome Financial Limitations

Traditional financial advice says, "Cut expenses" or "Get a second job." But creativity asks: "What do I enjoy doing that could also generate income?"

The creative approach:

- Identify what energizes you: I loved making people laugh, creating experiences, and bringing joy. Clown work wasn't draining. It was energizing.

- Look for skill overlaps: My hospitality skills (event management, customer service, performance under pressure) transferred perfectly to children's entertainment.

- Start with what you have: I didn't need a massive investment. Clown school, some supplies, a playlist, and my natural ability to entertain were enough to begin.

- Test with low risk: Starting with friends and family meant building my confidence and skills before investing heavily.

"You can only become truly accomplished at something you love. Don't make money your goal. Instead, pursue the things you love doing, and then do them so well that people can't take their eyes off you." Maya Angelou

Questions to ask yourself:

- What do I do that doesn't feel like work?

- What skills do I have that could generate income in unexpected ways?

- What creative solutions am I dismissing because they don't look "traditional"?

Understanding Your Transferable Skills Beyond Traditional Roles

The biggest financial restriction isn't lack of money; it's lack of imagination about how your skills can create value.

I thought my skills were tied to hospitality management, but I was skilled at:

- Creating memorable experiences

- Managing unpredictable situations

- Reading people and adapting quickly

- Performing under pressure

- Bringing joy to others

Those skills worked at a hotel front desk and at a five-year-old's birthday party.

How to identify your transferable skills:

- Look beyond your job title: What are you doing when you're working? Managing chaos? Building trust? Creating order? Solving problems?

- Notice what comes naturally: What do people consistently compliment you on or ask you for help with?

- Consider your whole life: Skills aren't just professional. Maybe you're great at organizing, mediating conflicts, teaching, or bringing people together.

- Think about what you'd do for free: Often our most valuable skills are things we enjoy so much we'd do them without pay.

My realization: I'd been thinking too narrowly about how to use my abilities. The same skills that made me a good hotel director made me a great children's entertainer, and they have now made me become a life coach full-time. Just like my decision to go to clown school, I started to train in life coaching and get one-on-one certification not just for additional financial benefit for my family but also to fulfill my purpose. I just had to see the connection.

Overcoming the Fear of Trying Something New

The biggest barrier to financial creativity isn't lack of ideas. It's fear of looking foolish, failing, or stepping outside established paths.

How I moved through the fear:

- **Reframed the story:** Instead of, "I'm giving up my professional identity," I told myself, "I'm expanding what's possible for me."

- **Started small:** Friends and family parties meant low stakes and high support.

- **Separated identity from income source:** Being a clown didn't make me less professional; it made me more versatile.

- **Focused on purpose over perception:** I was providing for my family and bringing joy. What others thought mattered less than what I needed to do.

The unexpected benefit: my willingness to try something unconventional, to not take myself too seriously, and to get creative about income were lessons that served me far beyond the extra money I earned. They taught me that financial restrictions are often mental restrictions about what's "acceptable" or "appropriate" for someone like me.

Moving Forward with Financial Restrictions

The Financial pillar teaches us that sustainable resource patterns aren't about maximizing income at any cost. They're about aligning how you make money with who you are and what you value.

For me, that meant:

- Stability: Consistent income that allowed flexibility

- Creativity: Additional income from work that energized rather than drained me

- Alignment: All income sources supported my purpose of caring for and bringing joy to children

The clown work didn't make me rich. But it taught me that financial limitations can be invitations to discover creative solutions I would never have considered if money hadn't been tight.

Key insights:

- Financial restrictions often reveal untapped creativity.

- Your skills are more transferable than you think.

- Fear of unconventional choices keeps us financially stuck.

- Purpose-aligned income is more sustainable than purely profit-driven work.

When you stop seeing financial limitations as walls and start seeing them as invitations to get creative about how you generate resources, everything changes.

Financial Space Reflection Worksheet: Understanding Your Financial Situation

Financial Restrictions to Identify

- Income limitations
- Debt load
- Savings gaps
- Financial literacy
- Money mindset issues
- Wage gaps (gender, race)
- Financial dependencies
- Wealth-building barriers

Red Flags: *(check all that apply)*

- ☐ You're living paycheck to paycheck.
- ☐ You avoid looking at your finances.
- ☐ You have no emergency fund.
- ☐ Money stress keeps you up at night.
- ☐ You don't know how to negotiate salary.
- ☐ You're financially dependent.

☐ You're drowning in debt.

Self-reflecting on the red flags you checked above:

How are these restrictions affecting your ability to pursue your purpose?

Identifying Creative Possibilities

1. What do you do that energizes you rather than drains you?

2. If money weren't an issue, what would you spend your time doing?

3. Looking at your answer above, is there any way to generate income from that activity?

Transferable Skills Assessment

1. Beyond your job title, what are you actually good at?

Core skills:

-
-

2. What do people consistently ask you for help with or compliment you on?

3. What skills from your professional life could be applied to completely different contexts?

Overcoming Fear

1. What unconventional income ideas have you dismissed? Why?

2. What financial choices are you avoiding because of what others might think?

3. Complete this statement:

"I would try _____ if I weren't afraid of _____."

Creative Income Exploration

1. In what low-risk way could you test a creative income idea this month?

2. Who in your network might need services or skills you naturally have?

3. What resources do you already have that could generate income?

Action Steps

1. What's one creative financial experiment you could try in the next 30 days?

2. What skill translation exercise will you practice this week? (Describe what you do in universal rather than industry-specific terms.)

3. What support do you need to overcome your fear and try something new financially?

Reflection Question:

If you weren't worried about what others might think, how would you creatively address your current financial restrictions

CHAPTER 10

The Purpose Pillar

PURPOSE PILLAR: Allowing your unique contribution to emerge and express itself

I've always known, since I was a young girl, that I wanted to help others. My leadership style has always been to rise up those around me. I've come to the realization that any business is what it is because of the people who work there. Simple math: happy staff = happy customers.

The question was always: How does the team stay happy? How do I keep them engaged as a leader? What do I want from my leaders?

From early in my career, I took pride in training and helping others reach their full potential and achieve their goals. I always seemed to attract team members who were eager to learn and grow. I created my own development plans tailored to the individual, had one-on-one meetings, and offered mentoring that was meaningful.

My greatest joy was seeing others around me achieve their goals.

"I've learned that people will forget what you said, people will forget what you did, but people will never forget how you made them feel." Maya Angelou

At one point in my career, I managed an all-female department head and assistant department head team. This wasn't purposeful but had happened organically. And those ladies thrived, a few getting promoted around the same time. I'm proud of the impact I made, and I can honestly say that I've built the best friendships based on my leadership and living my purpose.

Sometimes, we have to do things that have never been done. I paved the way at that iconic golf resort as the first female Latina to hold the position of Director of Rooms in its history. I'm proud to have created an annual International Women's History Month event for all the budding female leaders at the resort who wanted to hear stories of resilience and leadership in hospitality. They wanted the camaraderie, as well as the chance to discuss some of the restrictions they face as women in the industry.

As a woman, especially a Latina woman, in leadership, living my purpose meant navigating the restriction of being "the first." Being "the first" is simultaneously an honor and a burden: you're paving the way while knowing every decision you make reflects not just on you but on every woman who comes after you. The restriction wasn't my ability to lead; it was the weight of knowing that if I failed, doors might close for other women. If I succeeded, I could open them wider. That pressure to be excellent, to prove women belonged in these roles, to create space for those coming behind me—that was leading unrestricted. Not by ignoring the gender dynamics, but by using my position to change them.

The lesson: Living your purpose is really about understanding your why: understanding who you are in this present moment and who you want to be. It's about what legacy you want to leave.

What Purpose Space Teaches Us

The Purpose pillar isn't about finding your "one thing." It's about recognizing what naturally energizes you, what impact you want to make, and then aligning your life to create space for that contribution to emerge.

How to Identify Your Unique Contribution Beyond Roles and Titles

For years, I thought my purpose was tied to my job title. Director of Rooms. Department Head. Manager. But when I opened the daycare, or became a clown, or left hospitality entirely, my purpose didn't change. Only the context changed.

The shift I had to make:

From: "My purpose is what I do professionally."

To: "My purpose is how I show up, regardless of context."

What I discovered:

Whether I was training hotel staff, mentoring department heads, teaching at the daycare, or entertaining at birthday parties, the through line was always the same: "I help others rise."

That's my unique contribution. Not managing properties. Not leading teams. Not any specific job function. My core purpose is helping people discover and develop their potential.

How to identify your unique contribution:

- Look for patterns across different contexts: What are you doing when you feel most alive? Look for the common thread across seemingly different activities.

- Notice what people thank you for: Not just when they say, "Good job," but the moments when someone says, "You changed how I see myself" or "I couldn't have done this without you."

- Identify what you can't NOT do: What feels like breathing? What would you do even if no one paid you or recognized you for it?

- Ask: What change do I want to see? For me, it was watching people realize they're capable of more than they believed.

Questions to ask yourself:

- When do I feel most energized and fulfilled?

- What impact do I want to have on others?

- What would I want people to say about how I affected their life?

- What patterns show up across my different roles and experiences?

Strategies for Living Your Purpose While Meeting Practical Responsibilities

The restriction many women faces isn't discovering their purpose; it's finding space to live it while managing all the practical demands of life.

I knew my purpose was developing others, but I still needed to:

- Pay bills
- Care for my children
- Meet work deadlines
- Manage household responsibilities
- Handle career expectations
- Nurture my relationship as a wife

How I created space for purpose within practical constraints:

- Integrate, don't separate: I didn't wait for "someday" when I'd have time for my purpose. I integrated purpose into whatever I was already doing. Training staff at work. Mentoring my daughters. Supporting my sisters. Teaching at the daycare. Purpose wasn't separate from daily life; it was woven through it.

- Start where you are: I didn't need a perfect platform or the ideal role to live my purpose. Creating those individual development plans for team members? That was living my purpose. Having meaningful one-on-ones with the team members I managed? That was my purpose in action.

- Build purpose into your current role: When I became Director of Rooms, I didn't just manage operations. I built a team, and I built mentoring into my leadership structure. I made developing others a core part of how I defined success.

- Create small spaces for big impact: The all-female leadership team that thrived and got promoted together? That wasn't a massive program. It was consistent mentoring, tailored development plans, and intentional support. Small, consistent actions aligned with purpose create significant impact.

- Let purpose inform major decisions: When I chose the daycare over climbing higher in hospitality, purpose guided that choice. When I created the women's leadership event, purpose made it non-negotiable despite busy schedules.

Strategies for living purpose practically:

- Identify 10-minute purpose actions: What can you do in brief moments that aligns with your purpose? For me, this might be a meaningful conversation with a team member during lunch.

- Make purpose your lens for decisions: When faced with choices, ask yourself, "Which option creates more space for my purpose?"

- Track purpose impact, not just professional achievements: I measured success partly by how many people I helped develop, not just by operational metrics.

- Build community around shared purpose: The women's leadership event created space for collective purpose, making individual efforts more sustainable.

Ways to Measure Success by Impact Rather Than by Recognition

The restriction many women face is that living our purpose often means our greatest contributions go unrecognized. Development work is quiet. Mentoring happens behind closed doors. Helping others shine means we're often in the background.

What I learned about measuring success:

- The promotions of others became my milestones: When my all-female leadership team got promoted simultaneously, that was my success. Not my own next promotion but watching them rise.

- The conversations that changed trajectories: I don't remember most operational achievements. But I do remember the team member who told me, years later, that our conversations made her believe she could lead. That's the metric that matters.

- The ripple effect over immediate results: Creating the Women's History Month event wasn't immediately impressive on my resume. But knowing those women now have community, support, and inspiration? That's success that compounds over time.

- Legacy over recognition: Being "the first" female Latina Director of Rooms matters less than what comes after. Did I create space for more women to follow? Did I make it easier for the next person? That's the measure.

How to measure purpose-driven success:

- Track impact stories: Keep notes of moments when your purpose showed up. A mentee's breakthrough. A colleague's gratitude. A team member's promotion.

- Measure by whom you've helped rise: Success isn't your next position; it's how many people you've helped reach theirs.

- Notice the changes others don't see: The confidence someone gained. The goal someone set because you believed in them. The career path someone pursued after your mentoring.

- Value invisible work: The meeting where you advocated for someone's promotion. The development plan you tailored. The time you spent listening. This work is often invisible but profoundly valuable.

- Celebrate collective achievements: When your team succeeds, that IS your success. Their wins are evidence of your impact.

Moving Forward with Purpose Restrictions

The Purpose pillar teaches that living your purpose isn't about waiting for the perfect role, the right title, or complete freedom from responsibilities. It's about recognizing your unique contribution and finding ways to express it within whatever constraints you're currently experiencing.

Key insights:

- Your purpose exists beyond any single role or title.

- Living your purpose is about consistent small actions aligned with your why.

- Success is measured by your impact on others, not recognition for yourself.

- Purpose can be woven through daily responsibilities.

- Being "the first" carries the responsibility of creating space for those who follow.

When you understand your purpose, restrictions become less about what you can't do and more about how creatively you can express your contribution within the space you have.

For me, that purpose has remained constant: helping others rise, whether in hospitality, in a home daycare, at birthday parties, or creating women's leadership events. The context changes, but the contribution stays the same.

What's your unique contribution? What change do you want to create? What legacy do you want to leave?

Those questions will guide you through every restriction you face.

Purpose Space Reflection Worksheet: Understanding Your Purpose

Purpose Restrictions to Identify

- Unclear calling: you don't know what you're meant to do

- Fear of pursuing purpose

- Practical barriers to purpose work: real obstacles that prevent you from living your purpose

- Impostor syndrome: feeling like a fraud ("Who am I to do this?")

- Permission-seeking: waiting for someone to tell you it's okay

- Purpose vs. paycheck conflicts: your purpose doesn't pay your bills

- Legacy considerations: worrying about the impact you'll leave

- Contribution capacity: questioning if you have the energy, resources, or ability to contribute meaningfully

Red Flags: *(check all that apply)*

☐ You have no idea what your purpose is.

☐ You know your purpose, but you aren't living it.

☐ Fear is stopping you from pursuing your calling.

☐ You're waiting for permission.

☐ You feel like you're wasting your life.

☐ You envy others living their purpose.

☐ You feel as if you're running out of time.

Reflecting on any check marks above:

1. When do you feel most energized and alive? What are you doing in those moments?

2. What patterns show up across different areas of your life (work, family, friendships, hobbies)?

3. Complete this sentence: "I can't NOT

_____."

Identifying Your Unique Contribution

1. What do people consistently thank you for or seek you out for?

2. If you could change one thing in the world through your daily actions, what would it be?

3. What do you do that feels like breathing—so natural, you barely notice you're doing it?

4. Looking back at your life, what's the common thread across your most meaningful experiences?

Living Your Purpose Within Constraints

1. What practical responsibilities are you currently juggling?

2. Where could you integrate your purpose into what you're already doing?

3. What "10-minute purpose actions" could you take this week?

Purpose-Driven Decisions

1. What decision are you currently facing? How does each option align (or not) with your purpose?

2. Where might you be sacrificing purpose for recognition or status?

3. What would change if you made decisions based primarily on purpose alignment?

Measuring Impact

1. Who have you helped rise? List specific people and how you contributed to their growth.

2. What invisible work are you doing that creates real impact?

3. What stories of impact do you need to start tracking?

Legacy Planning

1. What do you want people to say about how you affected their life?

2. What path do you want to pave for those who come after you?

3. If you could only be remembered for one contribution, what would it be?

Action Steps

1. What's one way you can live your purpose more fully this week within your current circumstances?

2. Who's one person you could mentor, support, or help rise this month?

3. What purpose-aligned action have you been postponing? Why?

Reflection Question:

If you fully lived your purpose within your current restrictions (not waiting for the perfect circumstances), what would change about how you spend your time and energy?

CHAPTER 11

When All Eight Pillars Collapse at Once

The Compounded Restriction of Motherhood

Throughout this book, I've walked you through each pillar individually, showing you how restrictions in one area can become catalysts for movement. But life doesn't always restrict us one pillar at a time. Sometimes, a single event creates a cascading failure across every dimension of your life simultaneously.

Everyone faces their own situations where they may see a trickle effect in all areas of their life. The personal story I will share is from me wearing my mother hat. **Sometimes, the restriction isn't about your own movement—it's about creating space for someone else to find theirs.**

The Cascade: When One Restriction Triggers Eight

My youngest daughter was going back to in-person learning post-COVID, right at the beginning of junior high. Friend groups were already established from elementary school, and she was not only new to the school but new to the area. She was excited, nervous, and afraid all at the same time.

What I didn't know then was that the next two years would teach me everything about how the eight pillars interconnect, not just in my life but in hers too, and in how we navigated this restriction together.

She walked into that school bringing her whole authentic self: her Brooklyn confidence, her curly hair, her Italian/New Yorican culture, her style, her voice. And they tried to break her for it.

The bullying came in every form. Gender-based. Race-based. Academic undermining from teachers who should have protected her. I found myself questioning administrators on their decision-making, trying to understand how they couldn't see what was happening right in front of them. Then there were the teachers who made snide remarks via email when my daughter asked clarifying questions—but when I intervened? Suddenly, their tone changed.

This is what systemic restriction looks like. And as a mother, as a woman of color, as someone who'd moved her family across the country for "opportunity," I faced a compounding restriction that tied all eight pillars together: **I could see the problem clearly, but I couldn't fix it for her.**

The Synovial Space Assessment: Mapping the Cascade

In the Synovial Space methodology, we assess restrictions across all eight pillars to understand where movement is possible and where it's not. Here's what this single restriction—bullying at school—did to every dimension of my daughter's life, and mine:

Physical Pillar

- **Her restriction:** Stress manifested in her body as increased anxiety, sleep disruptions, and tension she carried in her shoulders.

- **My restriction:** Watching her suffer physically and feeling utterly helpless. My body carried the weight of her pain. I couldn't sleep either.

Mental Pillar

- **Her restriction:** She started doubting herself and questioning her identity. One teacher—a minority woman herself—responded to her clarifying questions with disgust. The mental repercussions of being undermined by someone who should have understood her experience created profound confusion.

- **My restriction:** The mental battle of wanting to intervene while knowing my daughter needed to find her way through this herself. Every day, I had to consciously choose: "Do I let her build resilience, or do I protect her from more harm?" That mental calculation never stopped.

Emotional Pillar

- **Her restriction:** Withdrawal. Confusion about her feelings. Learning to regulate emotions in an environment designed to destabilize her.

- **My restriction:** Balancing protection with creating space for her resilience. Separating my rage from her needs. Managing my own emotional response without making it her burden.

Spiritual Pillar

- **Her restriction:** Questioning fairness: "Why is this happening to me?" She was searching for meaning through suffering she didn't deserve.

- **My restriction:** Trying to help her find purpose through pain I couldn't take away. Trusting there was a reason she had to face this, even when I couldn't see it.

Professional Pillar

- **Her restriction:** Her future thinking shifted. She knew with absolute clarity: "I want to help others. I will never be like these teachers and administrators."

- **My restriction:** Professional identity crisis. I had moved us here for "better opportunities." Was this my fault? Had my career ambitions hurt my child?

Relational Pillar

- **Her restriction:** Trust eroded—in her friend group, in teachers, in administrators. This affected how much she shared at home, knowing Raphael and I wanted to "flip out on everyone."

- **My restriction:** I wanted to fix everything, but I had to let her lead the relationship and learn to be present without controlling, to offer support without smothering, and to rage privately while remaining steady for her.

Purpose Pillar

- **Her restriction:** She was learning to find her own path through bullying and bias, discovering her personal strength through adversity.

- **My restriction:** Letting her go to find herself. Trusting that this painful experience was shaping her purpose, even though every maternal instinct screamed to remove her from it immediately.

The Woman's Burden: The Compounding Restriction of Watching Your Child Suffer

Here's what they don't tell you about being a mother facing your child's restriction:

- **Society expects you to fix it.** Good mothers protect their children. Good mothers don't let their children suffer. Good mothers certainly don't move their children across the country into environments that harm them. The guilt was crushing.

- **But fixing it would have stolen her power.** If I'd swooped in immediately, fought all her battles, and removed her from every uncomfortable situation, I would have sent the message that she couldn't handle hard things. That she needed me to save her. That her strength wasn't enough.

The Synovial Space principle applies here too: Sometimes, the most loving thing you can do is create space within the restriction, not remove the restriction entirely.

My daughter was clear with me: "I want to handle this. I'll let you know if I need you to step in." She was teaching me the methodology I was teaching others: **assess the restriction, identify where movement is possible, and take strategic action within what you can control.**

Teaching the Methodology to the Next Generation

What I realized during those two years is that I wasn't just watching my daughter suffer. **I was watching her learn the Synovial Space methodology in real time.**

She was:

- **Assessing her restrictions** across all eight pillars

- **Identifying which pillars were most affected** (Relational, Emotional, Mental)

- **Making strategic decisions** about where to focus her energy

- **Creating movement** within impossible constraints (eventually switching to online school after moving out of California)

- **Building her own resilience** by choosing when to fight and when to conserve energy

The methodology worked because she owned it. Not because I imposed it.

The Three Critical Decisions: When All Pillars Are Restricted

When facing a cascade restriction (one event that impacts all eight pillars simultaneously) you have three choices:

Choice 1: Try to fix every pillar at once.

This is what mothers instinctively want to do: address the physical symptoms, the mental doubt, the emotional withdrawal, the spiritual crisis, all of it, immediately.

The problem: It's overwhelming. You can't create sustainable movement in eight dimensions simultaneously. You'd burn out trying to hold everything together.

Choice 2: Remove the restriction entirely.

In my case, this would have meant pulling her out of school immediately and moving back to New York. That is, eliminating the source of the problem.

The problem: Sometimes, the restriction is what teaches you. As much as it hurt, my daughter was learning something essential about herself, about injustice, and about her purpose. Removing the restriction would have removed the lesson.

Choice 3: Apply the Synovial Space methodology systematically

- Assess all eight pillars.
- Identify the two to three pillars most critical to address first.
- Create space for movement where it's possible.
- Support her in building her own resilience.
- Adjust the strategy as circumstances change.

We chose Choice 3. And it worked.

The Integrated Approach: Supporting Movement Across Pillars

Here's how we applied the methodology:

Priority Pillars (Immediate Focus)

1. **Emotional:** She needed tools to process what was happening.

2. **Mental:** She needed to separate her worth from others' treatment of her.

3. **Relational:** She needed to maintain connection with us even when she didn't want to share everything.

Support Actions

- Communication to process emotions and build coping strategies (Emotional)

- Reframing conversations: "This says everything about them and nothing about you" (Mental)

- Creating space for her to share on her timeline, not ours (Relational)

Strategic Movement

- Eventually switching to online school (Physical + Mental + Emotional relief)

By taking this approach, the cascade effect worked in reverse: Once we'd stabilized her Emotional and mental pillars, movement became possible in other areas. She could think clearly about her future. She could invest in relationships that mattered. She could see purpose emerging from pain.

The Outcome: Movement Still in Progress

My daughter graduated middle school. The high school in our zone would have meant facing most of the same students and administrators who'd failed her. Hence, we did what we'd learned through the Synovial Space methodology: **we assessed the restriction, identified where movement was possible, and advocated strategically.**

We went to the district level. We made our case. We fought for her to attend a different high school. And we won.

Her freshman year started with hope. A new environment. Different administrators. A chance to start fresh. She began to have a better outlook. She was enjoying the "typical" high school experience.

Then we moved again. After her sophomore year had started, we relocated to a new state—another professional opportunity, another family transition. We enrolled her in online school, and something unexpected happened: **she's thriving.**

Academically, she's excelling. She gets to focus on herself and her talents without the constant social navigation that drained her energy in traditional school. The middle school experience fundamentally changed her perspective on friends, education, and teen life. Online school gives her space to process that transformation without pressure to "perform" normalcy.

But here's the truth: we don't know what will come next.

Will she return to in-person school? Maybe. We're in a new state with a completely different environment. Maybe this fresh start, in a new place where no one knows her story, will feel different.

Or maybe online school is her path forward. Maybe she's discovering that learning doesn't have to look like everyone else's experience to be valid. Maybe she's creating her own definition of what education means.

This is what moving through restriction looks like. It's not always a neat resolution. Sometimes, it's an ongoing experiment in finding what works.

The Real Lesson: Movement Doesn't Mean "Fixed"

Here's what the Synovial Space methodology taught us through this experience: **Movement through restriction doesn't mean the pain is over or that everything is resolved. It means you're actively maneuvering within the constraints instead of being paralyzed by them.**

My daughter learned she could:

- **Recognize when an environment is harmful** (middle school)

- **Advocate for change** (different high school)

- **Adapt when circumstances shift** (moving to a new state)

- **Choose what serves her growth** (online school for now)

- **Leave the door open to future movement (**maybe in-person school later, maybe not)

And I learned:

- **I can't predict what's best for her** (I thought California would be perfect).

- **Systems sometimes fail kids** (and no amount of maternal advocacy changes that completely).

- **Supporting her means trusting her assessment of her own restrictions** (even when it means another transition).

- **"Thriving" doesn't always look like I imagined it would** (online school wasn't my first choice, but it's working for her).

What This Means for Your Restrictions

If you're facing a cascade restriction—one event impacting all eight pillars—think about what my daughter's ongoing journey teaches:

1. **Movement doesn't require a perfect solution.** We didn't "solve" bullying. We moved around it, through it, away from it. Each decision created new possibilities without erasing what had happened.

2. **You can create space while the restriction is still present.** She's still processing the middle school trauma. She's still figuring out trust and friendships. However, she's doing that work in an environment that gives her breathing room. That's the space we created.

3. **One form of movement can lead to unexpected paths.** Advocating for the high school change taught us we could challenge systems. That confidence made the move to a new state feel possible. That openness made online school a positive option instead of a last resort.

4. **Your child's restriction timeline is not yours.** I wanted her "healed" and back in traditional school immediately.

She needed time. She needed online school. She needed to explore what education could look like when it's not replicating the environment that hurt her. Her timeline matters more than my comfort.

5. **"Thriving" is personal and evolving**. Right now, thriving means academic excellence, personal focus, and freedom from social performance. Tomorrow, it might mean something different. That's allowed.

The Methodology in Real Time

This is the Synovial Space methodology applied to an ongoing restriction:

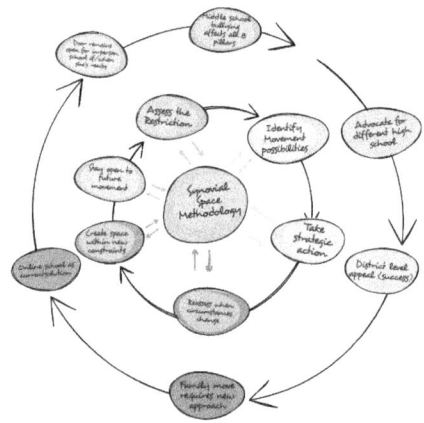

We're still in the middle of this story. We're still learning what works. We're still creating space for her to discover her own path.

And that's exactly what moving through restriction looks like when you're doing it right. It's messy, evolving, and deeply personal.

CHAPTER 12:

Your Toolkit

Sometimes, we face limitations or restrictions and we don't stop to reflect on them. We just keep moving full steam ahead, not taking time to see that there's an island blocking our path. How can we take time to recognize the restriction (island) and figure out if we still have an end goal of getting on the other side? How do we maneuver around this restriction (in this example, the island)? As one of my leaders told me, "Are you picking up what I'm putting down?" Aka, do you get what I'm saying?

This chapter is your toolkit. These are the practices I use. These are the frameworks I return to. This is how theory becomes action.

From Principle to Practice: Why Daily Movements Matter

Throughout this book, you've learned the Synovial Space principle: where there's restriction, there's the potential for movement. You've explored how this principle applies across all eight pillars of your life. You've seen how I've moved through restrictions in my career, my relationships, my body, my purpose. However, here's the truth that separates transformation from inspiration: Understanding the principle doesn't change your life. Practicing it daily does.

Think back to the biology. Synovial fluid doesn't create space in your joints through one dramatic moment. It works continuously, maintaining the gap between bones with every small movement you make. The space exists because of consistent, often invisible maintenance. Your life works in the same way.

The Compound Effect of Small Movements

When my daughters were being bullied, I didn't fix everything with one grand gesture. I created space through daily practices:

- Morning check-ins that gave them permission to share (or not share)

- Breathing exercises when anxiety spiked

- Evening reflections that separated my daughters' worth from others' treatment

Each practice was small. Some took 30 seconds. None were dramatic, but together, compounded over months, they created enough space for my daughters to find their own paths through the restrictions.

This is how movement happens. Not just through willpower alone. Not through one-time decisions but through daily practices that maintain the space between you and your restrictions.

Why Women Sometimes Need Structured Practices More Than Motivation

As women, we're often told we need more motivation, more inspiration, more self-care. However, motivation fades. Inspiration is fleeting. What you need are practices that work regardless of how you feel.

When I was on bed rest during my pregnancy, I didn't feel motivated. When my father died, I wasn't inspired. When my daughter was suffering, I was barely holding it together, but I had practices: small, repeatable actions I could take even when my emotional capacity was at zero.

The practices worked because they:

- Required no emotional energy: I could do them on autopilot when necessary.

- Created structure when everything else was chaos: When I couldn't control outcomes, I could control my 10-minute morning routine.

- Built evidence of my own capacity: Each day I practiced became proof I could keep moving.

- Maintained space in my joints when pressure was highest: Just like synovial fluid protects bones under stress, practices protect your well-being under pressure.

What This Chapter Will Give You

In the pages that follow, you will find:

- **The actual daily practices I use.** Not idealized versions but the real, quick routines that keep me grounded when life is chaotic

- **Decision frameworks for major life choices.** The process I used to leave my 20+ year career, including the Fight Pillar Impact Assessment and the Third Option Framework

- **Emergency protocols** for when everything collapses at once

- **Maintenance practices that prevent setback.** Weekly, monthly and quarterly reviews that catch small restrictions before they compound

The most important thing to remember: You don't need to do all these practices. You need to do the ones that create space in YOUR life.

Start with one. Build slowly. Adjust constantly. The goal isn't perfection. The goal is creating enough space to keep moving when restrictions appear. Just as synovial joints need different amounts of fluid depending on the activity (more when you're running and less when you're resting), your practices will shift based on what your life demands in any given season.

The toolkit isn't rigid. It's adaptive. Just like you.

Now let's build yours.

Tool 1: Daily Practices That Actually Work

Morning Routine: I'm going to give you a sneak peek into the first few minutes of my morning:

- After first greeting my husband, who I'm grateful for, I then...

- Make up my bed (new day, fresh start, new opportunity, start with a fresh neat environment to make me feel good).

- Open the blinds to let the sun in, giving me that morning energy.

- Flip the page over to the new day on my motivational calendar and see how it resonates in my life.

- I always have my nightstand next to my bed set up with some of my favorite grounding things (for example, a candle with an inspiring message, gemstones, a peppermint inhaler, a bright picture frame to give me energy and inspo).

- I either take a minute to meditate or pray, or I take one of my fun-colored pens where the colors always have meaning to me (for example, green for prosperity) and write whatever's on my mind, which is mostly giving gratitude. I've been writing in Spanish lately. It's just what comes in my mind first, even though English is my first language.

- When I was going to the hotel to work, I would either listen to music while getting ready to raise the vibration for the day or look up motivational videos on YouTube to get my mindset right for the day.

This quick routine works for my life as a woman/mom/professional because I'm setting myself up for the right emotional, physical, mental, and relational state right from the beginning of my day.

It prevents me from having initial negative thoughts that set the tone for the remainder of the day. Instead, I create a tone of positivity, opportunity, and gratitude.

Midday Reset: How I recalibrate during the workday.

These are the quick five- to ten-minute practices I use to reset. You can use some of these or create your own based on what will help you recalibrate. Everyone's different.

- Stretch: I stand up and move my body.

- Take a quick walk: It doesn't have to be long. I'm just letting the blood flow in my body.

- Get some air outside in nature: Reuniting with nature can be grounding.

- Breathe: I take deep breaths through my belly. I also use this technique to lower my blood pressure. It's a form of longer, slower breathing that can help calm the nervous system. To practice it, sit or lie comfortably, inhale slowly through your nose for five seconds, then exhale slowly through your mouth (or nose) for ten seconds, then repeat the cycle. The extended exhale is key for activating the body's relaxation response. This technique calms the nervous system, reduces stress and anxiety, and increases oxygen levels.

- Have a quick chat with someone who has positive vibes.

- Look at pictures in my phone photo album (happy memories).

- Read a positive post on social media.

- Read the "Daily Motivation" or "Daily Good" email (a volunteer-run initiative that delivers motivational messages or real-life inspirational stories). I get these daily, and they also include affirmations.

- Prayer: I ask my higher power to give me patience and strength to continue to move forward.

Timing is everything:

I use these strategies when I feel stressed, anxious, or overwhelmed. I remember a situation when I was at work and it was the beginning of the day. This was during that short stint I mentioned a few chapters earlier when I worked as a charter school teacher. I did my morning routine. I was feeling good.

My supervisor at the time was the principal of the school. She was watching me as I brought my class up from the school yard line-up. I'm a very free-spirited person, and I love for kids to be themselves, socialize, and use their creative juices. The class was too loud (according to the principal), so she told me in front of my class and other teachers that I needed to get my class under control. She reprimanded me right then and there in the hallway. For me, it was just the students' excitement about meeting up with their classmates and starting a new day. I didn't find them loud and rambunctious. They were seven- and eight-year-olds. It was natural for them to chitchat.

I was so angry that I'd been called out publicly in front of my students and peers. I felt that this was not the right thing for a leader to do. It messed up my flow and my morning vibes. I had to recalibrate. In that moment, I took a deep breath and thanked her for her feedback. Once I had a prep break, I went outside to get some air and take a quick walk. I needed to regroup so that my restriction wouldn't affect other areas in my life.

For example, in that moment when she spoke with me, I could feel my heart starting to race and my blood pressure rising, affecting my Physical pillar. This could have caused a domino effect on all of my pillars, because I wanted to tell her to "kick rocks," which would have affected my Financial, Professional, Relational, Mental, and Emotional pillars, all in the same moment. It's important to take a few minutes to recalibrate when you're feeling restricted in any area during your day.

My Evening Close:

Separating home time from work time is important to keep me well-rounded:

- I make sure to turn it off, meaning I mute my work email notifications and just focus on my family and on regrouping myself for the next day.

- I reach out to family or friends whom I may have been thinking about that day, or if I haven't heard from them in a while, I make sure to do a little check-in.

- Engaging with my family without distractions is important for me.

- Self-care before I go to bed is key (such as my face care routine).

- I reflect on my day: What restrictions did I face? What could I have done differently? What went really well today?

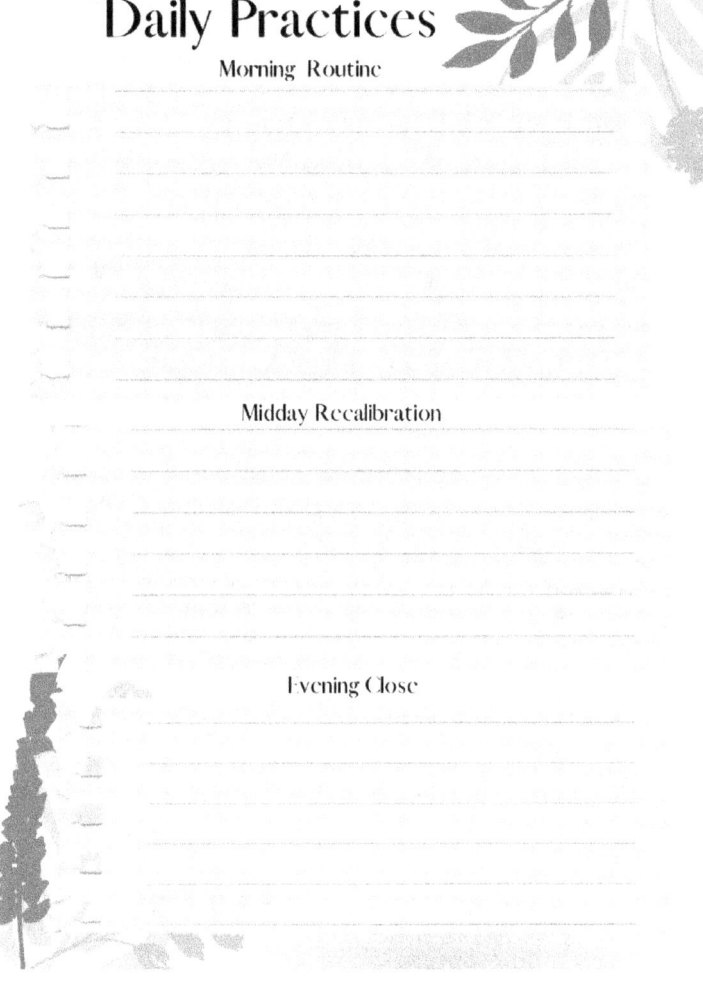

Daily Practices

Morning Routine

Midday Recalibration

Evening Close

Tool 2: Decision Frameworks for Real Life

The Story: September 4, 2025

Everything I've shared with you in the previous chapters—the frameworks, the insights, the movement—all comes down to daily practice. Theory means nothing without application.

On September 4, 2025, I moved back across the country to a new state and a new environment. I walked away from a 20+ year hospitality career. I was an Executive Committee member at a Southern California resort, managing 600+ guest rooms and villas, leading teams through 24/7 operations, and overseeing multimillion-dollar budgets. I'd trained over 1,000 staff members. I'd navigated constant constraints and earned respect.

And I left it all.

Not impulsively. Not in crisis. But through a deliberate decision-making process that took months and involved every framework I'm about to share with you.

This wasn't a "follow your passion and the money will follow" story. This was a systematic assessment of what staying would cost versus what leaving would make possible—across all eight pillars of my life.

Here's how I made the decision. These are the actual frameworks I used.

The Eight Pillar Impact Assessment

How to Use:

Utilizing the Eight Pillar Impact Assessment, my husband and I talked through each pillar to rate its current state, how it would be after we'd made the decision, and what the impact would be like: either positive or negative.

For any major decision, assess the impact across all eight pillars:

The Decision I'm Considering:

Sell our home/land and move closer to friends and family. Start our own business.

The Eight Pillar Impact Assessment

Pillars	Current State	After Decision	Net Impact +/-
Physical	Both my husband & I physically restricted/driving 5 hours daily/land work	Work out as a family	+better health
Mental	Mental exhaustion from managing the operations 10-12 hrs a day	Ability to focus on the future without thinking about the 24/7 operation	+peace of mind
Emotional	Fear of the unknown/guilt of leaving everything behind	Excitement about the possibility and walking into the unknown	+aligned with greater purpose
Spiritual	Disconnection between daily work and my greater purpose	Understand what is meant for me will be for me	+aligned with greater purpose
Professional	Not aligned with a profession that uses all of my skills full-time	Working full-time as a life coach helping clients navigate restrictions	+impact more people daily in a positive way
Relational	Relationships suffering because of work/life balance. Unable to speak to my daughter & East Coast family often because of the time difference	Strengthen relationships not just with my immediate family but also with extended family and friends because of proximity	+able to tighten the relationship with my family/friends
Financial	Financial hardship maintaining the land/hours of my job while taking care of our teen	Being able to potentially make more money than we currently have. Just need to pay bills at the very least.	+impact on our funds for travel
Purpose	My purpose was lived only part-time in the interactions with mentees, training, and making a difference with team members	Daily life fulfillment of living my life purpose in helping others move through restrictions	+living true purpose and inspiring others

The Eight Pillar Impact Assessment

Pillars	Current State	After Decision	Net Impact +/-
Physical			
Mental			
Emotional			
Spiritual			
Professional			
Relational			
Financial			
Purpose			

Analysis:

- Pillars that improve:

- Pillars that worsen:

- Net positive or negative:

- Is this trade-off worth it?

Tool 3: The Third Option (Beyond Binary Thinking)

Most people see two choices when facing a career restriction:

- Option 1: Stay miserable in the current job.
- Option 2: Quit with no plan and blow up your life.

I saw those two options for months. Neither felt right.

Then I discovered Option 3: Build the bridge before you burn anything.

Here's what that looked like for me:

2017: Got certified in life coaching WHILE still working in hotels:

- I didn't quit to pursue coaching.
- I explored coaching part-time to test if it resonated.

- This required investment in time and training costs, but I kept my income.

2017–2025: Did pro bono coaching on the side WHILE advancing in hospitality:

- Refined my skills with real clients
- Coached people to make a real impact in their lives
- Proved to myself this wasn't just a fantasy

2023–2025: Raphael and I started planning H2P Collective:

- Developed the business model
- Created the offerings
- Built the website
- Established the legal entity
- All while maintaining my salary

September 2025: Relocated from California to Florida for proximity to friends and family. Left hospitality with a business almost ready to launch:

- We moved and transitioned to an apartment in Florida.
- This gave us time to settle, reduce expenses, and finalize the business infrastructure instead of buying a home.
- Strategic evolution over eight years.

The Third Option Framework

When you're facing a binary decision, ask: "What if I don't have to choose between staying and leaving? What if I can build toward the new thing WHILE I'm still in the old thing?"

The steps:

1. Keep the current job (maintain income and stability).

2. Start exploring (get certified, take courses, test ideas on the side).

3. Build incrementally (create the foundation for what's next).

4. Reduce risk (relocate for lower expenses, save aggressively, eliminate debt).

5. Make the transition when the bridge is built, not when frustration peaks.

This framework requires:

- Patience: 12 months to several years (mine took eight years)

- Courage: Living in the uncertainty of "not yet"

- Strategy: Building while working means less time for rest

- Discipline: Not quitting prematurely when you're exhausted

But it gives you:

- Safety: You're not jumping without a net.

- Options: You're creating alternatives, not escaping.

- Wisdom: You're testing your idea before betting everything on it.

- Confidence: You know the new thing works before you leave the old thing.

YOUR TURN:

If you're considering a major transition, ask yourself:

What's the binary choice I think I'm facing?

- Option 1: _____

- Option 2: _____

What's the third option (building the bridge)?

Step 1 (what I can do NOW while staying):

_____

Step 2 (what I can build over 6–12 months):

_____

Step 3 (what reduces the financial risk):

_____

Step 4 (when I actually make the leap):

_____

Timeline: _____

Tool 4: Weekly Pillar Check-In

"The Sunday Space Assessment"

When to use: Every Sunday evening (or your chosen day of the week)

Time needed: 10 minutes

What you'll need: This worksheet, a pen, 10 quiet minutes

Every Sunday evening after my family goes to bed, I sit with my journal and rate my eight pillars. I'm not looking for perfection. I'm looking for patterns. If my Physical pillar drops two weeks in a row, I know I need to address it before it cascades into Mental or Emotional restrictions. This 10-minute practice has saved me from countless setback moments by catching small restrictions before they compound.

PART 1: Quick Pillar Rating

Rate each pillar from 1 to 10 (1 = severely restricted, 10 = flowing freely). Circle the direction: ↑ Improving ↓ Declining → Staying the same

Pillar	This Week	Last Week	Direction
Physical: body, energy, health			⇧ ⇩ ⇨
Mental: thoughts,			⇧ ⇩ ⇨

mindset, clarity			
Emotional: feelings, regulation			⇑ ⇓ ⇨
Spiritual: meaning, purpose, faith			⇑ ⇓ ⇨
Professional: work, career, calling			⇑ ⇓ ⇨
Relational: connections, boundaries			⇑ ⇓ ⇨
Financial: money, security			⇑ ⇓ ⇨
Purpose: contribution, legacy			⇑ ⇓ ⇨

PART 2: The Cascade Check

Which pillar is most restricted this week?

_____

Is this restriction affecting other pillars? If so, which ones?

Example: Physical restriction (exhaustion) → Mental restriction (can't focus) → Emotional restriction (irritable with family)

PART 3: Movement Recognition

What restriction did I move through this week? (Even small movements count!)

Which of the three choices did I make most often this week?

☐ Accept as final

☐ Fight directly

☐ Move through

What does this pattern tell me?

PART 4: Women-Specific Reflection

Where did I sacrifice my needs for others this week?

What boundary did I honor (or fail to honor)?

Where am I waiting for permission instead of moving?

Did I help another woman move through a restriction this week?

PART 5: One Small Movement

Based on my most restricted pillar, what's ONE small movement I can create this week?

When will I do this? (Be specific: day/time)

Who can support me in this?

Weekly Wins (Celebrate)

Three things I moved through this week (not accomplished, but moved through):

    1.

    2.

    3.

Date completed: _____

Next Sunday check-in: _____

Tool 5: Monthly Deep Dive

"The Monthly Movement Review"

When to use: The last Sunday of each month, or whatever day of the week works best for your schedule, but pick a day. Put it on your calendar. Set your reminders like it's a doctor's appointment.

Time needed: 30–45 minutes

What you'll need: Your last four weekly check-ins, this worksheet, coffee/tea (your favorite beverage), quiet space

My Practice

On the last Sunday of every month, I review my last four weekly check-ins and look for patterns. This is where I spot the restrictions I didn't see in the moment: the ones that show up repeatedly or cascade across pillars. I also celebrate movement I accomplished that felt invisible at the time. This practice has helped me make strategic pivots before small restrictions become major crises.

PART 1: Pattern Recognition

Looking at your four most recent weekly check-ins, which pillar showed up as most restricted most often?

What restriction kept showing up repeatedly this month?

Was this restriction:

☐ Temporary (circumstantial, will pass)

☐ Ongoing (chronic, requires long-term strategy)

☐ Self-created (thought patterns, choices I'm making)

☐ External (systemic, environmental, beyond my control)

PART 2: The Three Choices Review

Looking back at the restrictions you faced this month, tally how often you made each choice:

- Accept as final: _____ times

- Fight directly: _____ times

- Move through: _____ times

What does this pattern reveal about how you're approaching restrictions?

Is this serving you, or do you need to shift your approach?

PART 3: Skill Translation Check

What skill did I use in an unexpected way this month?

Example: Used hospitality training (reading the room) to handle a difficult family conversation

How can I apply this skill to my most restricted pillar?

PART 4: Women Leading Unrestricted

Where did I redefine success on my own terms this month?

What gendered expectation did I challenge or succumb to this month?

How did I support another woman's movement this month?

Where did I lead unrestricted despite a limitation?

PART 5: The Bridge Question (Third Option Check-In)

Am I building toward something new while maintaining stability?

☐ Yes → What am I building?

_____

☐ No → Do I need to be?

_____

If yes: How far along is my bridge?

☐ Just starting (exploring, learning, testing)

☐ Foundation laid (have a plan, some skills, small steps taken)

☐ Bridge halfway built (actively building, seeing progress)

☐ Almost ready to cross (nearly ready to make the leap)

What's my next step in building this bridge?

PART 6: 90-Day Goal Review

What were my goals for this month?

     1.

     2.

     3.

Which ones did I achieve/make progress on?

Which ones stalled? Why?

Were my goals about achievement or movement? (Be honest.)

PART 7: Cascade Analysis

Did restriction in one pillar create unexpected movement in another?

Example: Financial restriction (daycare income lower) → Purpose movement (being with my child while taking good care of other children)

What does this teach me about how my pillars interconnect?

PART 8: Next Month's Movement Strategy

Based on this month's data, what needs to change in the next 30 days?

Which pillar needs the most attention?

What's ONE strategic movement I can create next month?

What support do I need to make this happen?

Monthly Celebrations

Three significant movements I created this month:

1.

2.

3.

One woman I helped rise:

One restriction I'm grateful for (because of what it taught me or created):

Month reviewed: _____

Next monthly deep dive: _____

Tool 6: Quarterly Recalibration

"The Seasonal Movement Strategy"

When to use: Last week of March, June, September, and December

Time needed: 45–60 minutes

What you'll need: Your last three monthly reviews, this worksheet, quiet uninterrupted time

My Practice

Every quarter, I take a full hour to step back and see the bigger picture. This is where I assess whether my daily movements are creating the life I actually want—or if I'm just surviving. I've made some of my biggest life decisions during these quarterly sessions: opening the daycare, returning to hospitality, leaving my 20+ year career. This practice helps me lead strategically, not reactively.

PART 1: The Big Picture Assessment

Looking at the past three months across all eight pillars:

Which pillar(s) had the MOST movement?

What created that movement?

Which pillar(s) stayed STUCK?

Why? What's keeping it restricted?

☐ I'm accepting it as final.

☐ I'm fighting it but making no progress.

☐ I haven't found the right way to move through it yet.

☐ External circumstances genuinely outside my control.

☐ I'm afraid to move.

☐ Other:

Overall Pillar Health (Rate each pillar's average over the quarter):

Pillar	Average Rating (1–10)	Trend This Quarter
Physical		☐ Improving ☐ Declining ☐ Stable
Mental		☐ Improving ☐ Declining ☐ Stable
Emotional		☐ Improving ☐ Declining ☐ Stable
Spiritual		☐ Improving ☐ Declining ☐ Stable
Relational		☐ Improving ☐ Declining ☐ Stable
Professional		☐ Improving ☐ Declining ☐ Stable

Financial		☐ Improving ☐ Declining ☐ Stable
Purpose		☐ Improving ☐ Declining ☐ Stable

PART 2: The Cascade Review

How did my pillars interact this quarter?

Restriction in _____ pillar created unexpected movement in _____ pillar.

Example: Daughter's bullying (Relational restriction) → Purpose clarity (I will help others facing injustice).

What does this teach me about how my life interconnects?

Is there a pillar that, when improved, tends to lift all the others?

That's your leverage point. Focus there next quarter.

PART 3: Purpose Alignment Check

Am I living my purpose WITHIN my current restrictions or waiting for restrictions to disappear?

☐ Living it now (integrated into daily life despite constraints)

☐ Waiting for "someday" (when the circumstances are perfect)

☐ Unsure what my purpose even is

If waiting: What's one way I could express my purpose THIS WEEK within my current life?

Looking at how I spent my time/energy this quarter, does it reflect my stated purpose?

☐ Yes, aligned

☐ Somewhat aligned

☐ Not aligned at all

If not aligned: What needs to change?

PART 4: Women Leading Unrestricted

This quarter, where have I been leading unrestricted?

What restriction am I treating as permanent that might actually be temporary?

Where have I:

- Redefined success on my own terms?

  _____

- Challenged gendered expectations?

  _____

- Created space for other women?

  _____

- Translated my skills in unexpected ways?

  _____

The Hard Questions:

Where am I performing a version of myself to fit expectations instead of being authentic?

What's the cost of that performance?

What would change if I fully trusted myself?

What am I afraid will happen if I lead completely unrestricted?

Is that fear based on reality or internalized messaging?

PART 5: The Third Option Progress

Am I building a bridge to something new while maintaining stability?

☐ Yes

☐ No

☐ I should be, but I'm not

If yes:

What bridge am I building?

Progress this quarter:

☐ Explored options (researched, networked, learned)

☐ Got certified/trained (invested in skills)

☐ Tested small (pilot projects, pro bono work, experiments)

☐ Built infrastructure (LLC, website, systems, savings)

☐ Generated income (monetized the new thing)

☐ Ready to cross (prepared to make the leap)

Milestones reached this quarter:

    1.

2.

3.

What's my timeline for crossing this bridge?

What do I need to have in place before I cross?

PART 6: Who Have I Helped Rise?

List the people you mentored, supported, or helped move through restrictions this quarter:

1.

2.

3.

How did helping them rise affect my own sense of purpose?

Am I measuring my success by THEIR growth, not just my own advancement?

☐ Yes

☐ No

☐ Sometimes

PART 7: Strategic Pivots for Next Quarter

Based on this quarter's data, what needs to change in the next 90 days?

Which pillar gets priority focus next quarter?

Why this one?

What's the ONE major movement I want to create in the next 90 days?

What would success look like? (Be specific)

Potential obstacles:

     1.

     2.

     3.

How I'll move through them:

     1.

     2.

     3.

PART 8: Support Systems

Who do I need in my corner next quarter?

•Mentor/coach:

_____

•Accountability partner:

_____

•Therapist/counselor:

_____

•Financial advisor:

_____

•Medical support:

_____

•Friend/sister circle:

_____

What support am I NOT asking for that I actually need?

Why am I not asking?

What would change if I asked?

PART 9: Quarterly Celebration

Major movements this quarter:

Three significant restrictions I moved through:

    1.

    2.

     3.

Three ways I led unrestricted:

     1.

     2.

     3.

Bridges I built:

Skills I translated:

Restrictions that became catalysts:

What I'm most proud of:

Letter to Myself 90 Days from Now:

Write a short note to the woman you'll be next quarter. What do you want her to know? What do you hope she's achieved? What do you want her to remember about this moment?

Quarter reviewed: _____

Next quarterly recalibration: _____

Signature: _____

Date: _____

TOOL 7: Emergency Restriction Protocol

"When You're Paralyzed by Restriction"

This is your lifeline when everything feels impossible.

Cut this page out, or print it. Keep it somewhere visible. Use it when you can't think clearly.

When to use this protocol:

- You're overwhelmed and can't move.
- A setback just hit.
- Everything feels like it's collapsing at once.
- You don't know what to do next.
- You're paralyzed by fear, grief, or exhaustion.

STEP 1: Breathe

(Your body needs oxygen before your brain can think.)

Do this RIGHT NOW: Sit or lie comfortably, inhale slowly through your nose for five seconds, then exhale slowly through your mouth (or nose) for ten seconds, repeating the cycle.

STEP 2: Name It

(You can't move through what you can't name.)

Which pillar(s) are restricted right now? (Check all that apply)

☐ Physical (body, health, energy, pain)

☐ Mental (thoughts spiraling, can't focus, confusion)

☐ Emotional (overwhelmed, numb, grief, rage)

☐ Spiritual (meaningless, lost, disconnected)

☐ Professional (job loss, conflict, failure)

☐ Relational (breakup, betrayal, loss)

☐ Financial (crisis, debt, income loss)

☐ Purpose (lost, stuck, unclear)

In one sentence, what just happened?

STEP 3: Assess

(Not all restrictions are permanent.)

Is this restriction:

☐ Temporary → This will pass. I need to survive this moment.

☐ Ongoing → This is chronic. I need a long-term strategy.

☐ Cascading → One restriction is triggering others.

Can I control the outcome?

☐ Yes, partially

☐ No, this is beyond my control

STEP 4: Choose

(You have three choices. Pick one.)

Right now, in this moment, I choose to:

☐ Option 1: Accept this as final. Sometimes, survival means accepting what is. There's no shame in this.

I accept that _____ is beyond my control

I will focus my energy on

_____

☐ Option 2: Fight this directly. Sometimes, the restriction must be confronted head-on.

I will fight by:

_____

First action I'll take:

_____

Who can help me fight:

_____

☐ Option 3: Move through this. I can't eliminate the restriction, but I can create movement within it.

I can't control _____,

but I can control _____.

The smallest movement I can create right now is:

_____.

STEP 5: Act

(Even the smallest movement breaks paralysis.)

What's the smallest movement I can make RIGHT NOW (in the next 10 minutes)?

Pick ONE:

☐ Call someone who loves me

☐ Drink water/eat something

☐ Take a five-minute walk

☐ Cry (emotion is movement)

☐ Write what I'm feeling

☐ Pray/meditate/sit in silence

☐ Take my medication

☐ Cancel something nonessential

☐ Ask for help

☐ Other:

_____

I will do this NOW.

STEP 6: Don't Do This Alone

(You're not meant to move through an emergency by yourself.)

Who can I reach out to RIGHT NOW?

Emergency contact 1: _____

Phone: _____

Emergency contact 2: _____

Phone: _____

Emergency contact 3: _____

Phone: _____

Professional support:

- Therapist: _____
- Phone: _____
- Doctor: _____
- Phone: _____
- Crisis hotline: call or text 988 (Suicide & Crisis Lifeline)
- Domestic violence: 1-800-799-7233
- Other: _____
- Phone: _____

STEP 7: Anchor to Truth

(When everything is chaos, remember what's true.)

Read these aloud:

√ This restriction does not define me.

√ I have moved through hard things before.

√ I don't need to fix everything today.

√ It's okay to not be okay right now.

√ Asking for help is a strength, not a weakness.

√ I am allowed to move slowly.

√ This feeling will not last forever.

√ I can create movement even when I can't create a solution.

NEXT 24 HOURS:

In the next 24 hours, I will:

1. Stabilize:

_____

(sleep, eat, hydrate, take medication, get to safety)

2.Reach out:

_____

(call one person, schedule one appointment, ask for one thing)

3.One small movement:

_____

(the tiniest step forward in my most restricted pillar)

REMEMBER:

You don't need to move through this perfectly. You don't need to move through this fast. You just need to keep moving.

Even the smallest movement through restriction is still movement.

I used this protocol on: _____

It helped me:

_____

I've used this protocol in hospital waiting rooms, after devastating phone calls, and in moments when I couldn't see any path forward. It works because it's simple enough to use when your brain won't work. You don't need to be strong to use this. You just need to breathe. Start there.

IF YOU'RE IN IMMEDIATE DANGER:

- Call 911

- Go to your nearest emergency room

- Call the National Suicide Prevention Lifeline: 988

- Text "HELLO" to 741741 (Crisis Text Line)

CHAPTER 13:

Leading Forward

Paying It Forward and Moving Forward

In 20+ years of hospitality leadership, I trained over 1,000 staff members. However, the numbers weren't what mattered. It was the development of women whom others had overlooked, under-estimated, or dismissed that made a profound impact on my life.

I noticed a pattern: **The women who came to me facing the steepest restrictions often had the greatest potential.**

They were facing restrictions others saw as disqualifying. Some were labeled "too stern" for leadership. These were women who cared deeply about people but were afraid to show it. As a female leader, they didn't want to be seen as "too weak." But in hospitality, caring about people is not a weakness. It's the entire point. I helped coach them on how to frame their emotional intelligence as strategic relationship-building, how to name their strength instead of apologizing for it, and how to find the appropriate balance while still being authentically genuine.

Others had the technical skills but had internalized messages that they weren't "leadership material." They'd start every contribution with, "I'm sorry, but..." or "This might be stupid, but..."

Mentoring and coaching helped them reframe their expertise. There was a lot of self-doubt: "I'm not good enough". I showed them how to pick their head up and be confident: "You have information we need. Speak it confidently."

I created development plans tailored to each woman's specific restrictions:

- Regular one-on-one meetings where we didn't talk just about work but about their whole lives, which included caregiving demands, work–life balance, financial pressures, and impostor syndrome.

- Stretch assignments that others thought they weren't "ready" for.

- Advocacy in rooms they weren't in. This came when promotions were discussed and when high-visibility projects were assigned, and their names needed to be on the list. I was their cheerleader.

The pattern was consistent: Each woman I helped mentor had capability that others overlooked because of bias: gender, race, language, style, age, something that made decision-makers hesitate. My job wasn't to create their competence. It was already there. My job was to see it clearly, create space for it to develop, and advocate for opportunities that matched their actual potential.

Where are they now?

Some are on executive teams, some are department heads. Others are Assistant Directors preparing for their next move. Several are running operations at different companies in fields such as hospital food services, nursing homes, timeshare, tech companies, and more.

What this meant to me:

Watching these women rise wasn't just professionally satisfying. It was purpose-fulfilling. Every promotion, every time one of them spoke up confidently in a meeting, every moment they stopped apologizing for their expertise was part of my success. Not my title. Not my salary. Their movement through restrictions they were told defined their ceiling.

The realization:

This is when I understood that my restrictions weren't just my own to navigate. They were preparation for helping others navigate theirs. Every barrier I'd moved through gave me a map I could share. Every time I'd been unspoken-ly told, "That position would be better for a man," every time I'd had to prove myself when competence was assumed in others, every time I'd navigated systems designed without women in mind—all of it had prepared me to help other women do the same.

The responsibility became clear:

When you've moved through restrictions that stop others, you don't get to keep that knowledge to yourself. You have an obligation to throw the rope back down. To open doors. To tell the truth about what it takes. To advocate loudly. To develop intentionally. To believe in women's potential even when systems don't.

This chapter is about that responsibility, and about how you can fulfill it. Whether you're a CEO or an entry-level employee. Whether you're managing teams or just starting your career. Whether you have formal authority or just the influence that comes from your own lived experience.

Because here's what I know: every woman who's moved through restriction has something to teach. Every woman who's negotiated barriers has a map that could help someone else. And every woman who's made it to the other side has a responsibility to make the path clearer for those still climbing.

The Responsibility of Moving Through When You've Made It Through

When you've moved through restrictions that stop others, you have a responsibility. Not because you're superior, but because you have information that could help.

I didn't do this alone. People opened doors, gave me opportunities, and advocated, mentored, and believed in me when I couldn't see my own potential.

My sisters never questioned my "crazy ideas." When I said I wanted to open a daycare, they didn't ask, "Are you sure?" They asked, "How can I help?"

My colleagues who became friends amplified my voice in meetings, credited my ideas when others tried to claim them, and celebrated my wins as their own.

What they taught me: Investment in another woman's success doesn't diminish your own. It multiplies it.

Your commitment: Every woman who moves through restrictions has a responsibility to throw the rope back down. To tell the truth. To open doors. To say, "Here's how I did it—and here's what I wish someone had told me."

Your Mentorship Opportunity

You don't have to be perfect to help.

My mentorship approach comes directly from my restrictions. I mentor the way I wish I'd been mentored.

Principle #1: See the Whole Person

What this means:

- Understand their restrictions, not just their performance.
- Account for their full context (work and personal life).
- Don't judge.
- Support their unique path.

How to apply it: Ask, "What restrictions is this person facing that I can't see?" Then design your support around their reality, not your assumptions.

Principle #2: Create Real Opportunities

Advice is cheap. Access is priceless.

What this means:

- Not just advice, but access
- Opening actual doors with your influence
- Taking calculated risks on people
- Using your position for others' advancement

How to apply it: Ask, "Who deserves an opportunity they're not getting?" Then use whatever influence you have to create it.

Principle #3: Teach Navigation, Not Just Skills

I taught my mentees how to navigate union environments, how to read political dynamics, how to advocate for themselves in ways that would be heard. I shared the unwritten rules I'd learned the hard way.

What this means:

- Political realities
- Unwritten rules
- Strategic moves
- Self-advocacy skills

How to apply it: Don't just teach the work. Teach how to navigate the system.

Principle #4: Model Imperfection

What this means:

- Share real stories, not just highlights.
- Admit mistakes and what you learned.
- Show the messy middle, not just the success.
- Normalize struggle as part of growth.

How to apply it: Be strategically vulnerable. Let them see your humanity.

Your Action Plan: From Inspiration to Action

Everything you've learned in this book means nothing without action.

Your Immediate Next Steps:

In the next 24 hours:

1.Name your most restricted pillar right now:

_____

2.Identify one small movement you can create:

_____

3.Who can support you: _____

In the next 7 days:

1.Complete your first Weekly Pillar Check-In (Tool 4).

2.Reach out to one woman who might need mentorship or advocacy.

3.Share one lesson from your restrictions with someone who needs to hear it.

In the next 30 days:

1.Complete your first Monthly Deep Dive (Tool 5).

2.Advocate for one woman in a room she's not in.

3.Make one systemic change in your sphere of influence, even if it's small.

In the next 90 days:

1.Complete your first Quarterly Recalibration (Tool 6).

2.Develop a mentorship relationship with one woman.

3.Take one strategic risk on someone others are overlooking.

Your mentorship map:

Women I could mentor:

1.

2.

    3.

What I could specifically offer each one:

    1.

    2.

    3.

One action I'll take this month:

Your advocacy commitment:

Who needs my advocacy right now?

What specific action will I take?

When?

Your Unrestricted Future

What "Unrestricted" Really Means

Let's be clear: "unrestricted" doesn't mean "without limitations." It means:

- Moving through restrictions instead of being stopped by them
- Using limitations as catalysts instead of excuses
- Creating possibility within constraints
- Building the life you want WITH your restrictions, not despite them

Your Five-Year Vision

If you keep creating movement the way this book teaches, and continue working with your restrictions, not against them, what becomes possible?

Reality Check: (keep the below questions in mind as you answer for each pillar)

For each vision, ask:

1. Does this account for my actual limitations?

2.Does this require circumstances I can't control?

3.Could I create movement toward this starting tomorrow?

4.Am I working WITH restriction or pretending it doesn't exist?

Physical Pillar:

Five years from now, my physical reality looks like:

Mental Pillar:

Five years from now, my mental capacity looks like:

Emotional Pillar:

Five years from now, my emotional health looks like:

Spiritual Pillar:

Five years from now, my spiritual life looks like:

Professional Pillar:

Five years from now, my career looks like:

Relational Pillar:

Five years from now, my relationships look like:

Financial Pillar:

Five years from now, my finances look like:

Purpose Pillar:

Five years from now, my contribution looks like:

Your Commitment

The Contract with Yourself

Everything you've learned means nothing without commitment. Not commitment to perfection. Commitment to movement.

Your Declaration:

I, _____, commit to:

Moving through my restrictions by:

Even when:

I will not:

- Accept restrictions as final without exploring movement

- Fight every battle at the cost of my well-being

- Navigate this alone when support is available

- Wait for perfect conditions before I start

I will remember:

- Movement doesn't mean perfect.

- Small movements compound.

- My restrictions prepare me to help others.

- I am not alone.

I will ask for help when:

I will celebrate:

I will be gentle with myself when:

Signature: _____

Date: _____

Witness/Accountability Partner (optional):

_____

The Ripple Effect: Your Movement Creates Movement

This isn't just about you. When you move through restriction, you show others it's possible. When you create movement, you give others permission.

My youngest daughter watched how I approached her bullying situation. She saw me assess the restriction, identify where movement was possible, and support her in building her own resilience rather than fixing everything for her.

Now she's thriving in online school, not because I removed every obstacle but because she learned she could move through them. She watched me lead unrestricted, and it gave her permission to do the same.

Your Legacy

What do you want to be true because you moved through your restrictions?

For my children:

For my community:

For women who come after me:

For myself:

FINAL MESSAGE

Standing at the Empire State Building

When Raphael proposed to me on top of the Empire State Building, he said we could see everywhere we'd been and beyond: where we were headed. Every time we'd see that building, whether in pictures, in movies, or from anywhere in the city, we'd remember our history was etched on that rooftop.

That's what I want for you.

I want you to look back at where you've been. Look at the restrictions you've moved through, the movement you've created, and know that your history is etched into who you're becoming. Not despite your limitations. Because of them.

Here's what I know:

- Restrictions aren't walls. They're doorways.
- You don't have to wait for perfect conditions to start moving.
- Small movements compound into transformation.
- You're not alone in this.
- Your story matters.
- The women coming behind you need to see you lead unrestricted.

So, Here's My Question:

What will you do with your unrestricted future?

What movement will you create? What restrictions will you move through? Who will you help along the way?

The women who came before us paved the way. Now it's our turn to lead unrestricted.

How to Continue

Join the community:

- H2P Collective Corp.: www.h2pcollective.com: For assessments, self-directed courses, downloadable handbooks, and more
- Connect:
  - Website:

    www.h2pcollective.com

    Instagram:@h2pcollective
  - Email: lstjames@h2pcollective.com

Continue your learning:

- Read: Synovial Space: A Guide to Dynamic Living by Raphael St James
- Share: Your own stories of moving through restrictions
- Mentor: At least one woman who needs what you've learned

A Note of Gratitude

Thank you for trusting me with your time and attention. Thank you for your willingness to look honestly at your restrictions. Thank you for choosing movement.

I can't wait to see what you create.

With love and respect,

Liz St James

The women who came before me paved the way. Now is our turn to lead unrestricted.

www.ingramcontent.com/pod-product-compliance
Lightning Source LLC
Chambersburg PA
CBHW060912120626
46553CB00001B/300